HOW TO PROTECT YOURSELF FROM IDENTITY THEFT

ENFIELD LIBRARIES

HOW TO PROTECT YOURSELF FROM IDENTITY THEFT

Elizabeth Drake

First published in Great Britain 2009

Apart from any fair dealing for the purpose of research or private study, or criticism or review, as permitted under the Copyright, Designs and Patents Act 1988, this publication may only be reproduced, stored or transmitted, in any form or by any means, with the prior permission in writing of the publisher, or in the case of reprographic reproduction in accordance with the terms and licences issued by the Copyright Licensing Agency. Enquiries concerning reproduction outside those terms should be addressed to the publisher. The address is below:

GLOBAL PROFESSIONAL PUBLISHING Limited
Random Acres
Slip Mill Lane
Hawkhurst
Cranborne
Kent TN18 5AD

www.gppbooks.com

GLOBAL PROFESSIONAL PUBLISHING believes that the sources of information upon which the book is based are reliable, and has made every effort to ensure the complete accuracy of the text. However, neither GLOBAL PROFESSIONAL PUBLISHING , the author nor any contributor can accept any legal responsibility whatsoever for consequences that may arise from errors or omissions or any opinion or advice given.

© Global Professional Publishing 2009
ISBN: 978-1-906403-04-1

London Borough of Enfield	
91200000028982	
Askews	~~May~~ June-2009
364.1633	£14.99
Y	

www.gppbooks.com

CONTENTS

Introduction 1

Part One How Your Information Gets Stolen. 5
    Shoulder Surfing 7
    Bin Raiding 7
    Mail Intercept 7
    Property Theft. 8
    ID Theft at the Workplace 8
    Telephone Fraud 8
    Internet Fraud 9
    Phishing. 9
    Public records. 9
    Skimming. 10
    Spyware 10
    E-mail scams. 10
    Early Warning Signs 15
    Responsiveness. 19
    Persistence 20
    Initiative 20
    Resourcefulness 20
    The Emotional Toll 22
    Credit Card Companies and Theft Protection. 28
    Privacy Policies 34

Online Banking...39
Peer-to-Peer (P2P) File Sharing 45
Voice Over Internet Protocol (VoIP) 51
Online Shopping: Is the Internet Safer than Mail?........57
E-Mail Scams 63
Phishing 69
Spyware and Adware 76
New Threats to Online Security 82

Part 2 Different Forms of Theft......................91
Individual Identity 92
The Solutions..96
Financial, Account Takeover, New Account Set-Up 98
The Solutions...101
National Insurance Number 103
The Solutions...107
Business Identity Theft 109
The Solutions... 113
Theft of Your Children's Information.................. 115
The Solutions... 119
Mortgage Fraud & Identity Theft.......................122
The Solutions...126
Bankruptcy Fraud & Identity Theft....................128
The Solutions... 131
International Identity Theft..........................133
The Solutions...137

Part 3 Future Protection 141
Protect Yourself While Travelling Internationally 141

The Solutions	145
The New Services Banks Provide	148
The Solutions	150
Your Credit Report	152
The Solutions	156
Identity Theft Insurance–Is It Worth the Money?	158
The Solutions	161
Setting-Up Fraud Alerts	164
The Solutions	166
Maximizing Computer Protections	170
The Solutions	173
Protecting Your Passwords & Choosing Secure Passwords	175
The Solutions	179
Back-Up Important Files	182
The Solutions	185
Active Duty Alerts for Military Personnel	189
The Solutions	192
Credit Monitoring Services	194
The Solutions	197
Part 4 Learn Who to Contact if Something Goes Wrong	**201**
The Solutions	203
Talking to the Right People	207
The Solutions	209
Identity Theft Complaints and Notices	212
The Solutions	215
Closing Compromised Accounts	218
The Solutions	221

Filing a Police Report 224

Organising Your Case Notes 228

The Solutions...230

How to Set-Up a System to Monitor Your Accounts and
Finances 233

The Solutions...236

Who Is Responsible for Losses When Theft Occurs? 239

The Solutions...243

Identity Theft Affidavit 246

The Solutions...250

Remedying Identity Theft Problems 253

Index *281*

INTRODUCTION

▌▌▌

Can you imagine coming home from work, sitting down and opening the day's mail and looking at your charge card bill to see that not only is it to the maximum, but over the credit limit! You scan down the list of charges and find boutiques, pricey restaurants and Websites–none of which, of course, you have ever even stepped foot in or gone to in your life. You sit and stare at the statement wondering what happened, when, and how.

Your first reaction is to rush to see if the credit card is in your wallet. Thankfully, it is, but what are these erroneous charges and what can you do about all of this? After fury turns to general anger, you begin to rationalise the process, wondering what else is going on. What about bank accounts and the mutual funds that you have had for years? You rush to your office and get online to see what the status is of your other charge and store cards. You do the same for every account you can get to immediately.

As every person who has ever had a pin number or credit card or even their entire identity stolen, this is the most frustrating and humiliating experience. Someone has not only used your good credit and financial resources to their advantage, but they have access to your purchases and your personal history. It is as much a violation as if they had knocked down the door and ransacked your home. To make matters worse, you have no real understanding as to how long it is going to take to get all of this settled. At the very least you will need to:

- Check and correct bank records;
- check and correct credit and store charge cards;
- check and correct mortgage and home equity accounts; and
- have repeated conversations and send letters with the three principle credit agencies to ensure that this information is not on your records.

All of this can and should be prevented if you use the enormously helpful tips provided in *Tips to Preventing Identity Theft*. Curing identity theft begins with preventing it in the first place. You will learn how to set-up simple systems to monitor your accounts, how to work with a credit company to prevent problems, what to do if you become an identity theft victim and how to manage your records and more.

Identity theft is nasty, brutish and very costly to cure. Stop thieves in their tracks and stop them now.

Everything you need is here to ensure your personal and financial safety.

Elizabeth Drake

Part One

HOW YOUR INFORMATION GETS STOLEN

In this information age, it has become quite easy for a criminal to steal your identity. Identity theft is the most common type of consumer fraud and is also the number one source of consumer complaints. Recent studies have shown that one in four individuals has been a victim of some form of identity theft and approximately 7 million people are victims of identity theft each year. New data released by credit-checking agency Experian reported a 69 percent increase in identity theft complaints in 2006 as compared to the same period just 1-year earlier.

Although no one is immune to becoming a victim of identity theft, some demographic groups may be at greater risk than others. Interestingly, seniors may represent only 10 percent of victims. It seems that individuals 18 to 39 are at greatest risk, representing about 52 percent of cases. Within that group, individuals 30 to 39 have the highest risk. There are many likely reasons for the vulnerability of these younger consumers. First and foremost, they represent a disproportionate percentage of Internet use–and Internet commerce–in this country. Also, typically, their incomes are rising as are their need to make purchases. First apartments, followed by first homes, need to be furnished. Weddings and the birth of children are also typically accompanied by a tremendous flurry of purchases.

But how does identity theft happen? The methods may be as sophisticated as stealing computer information or as crude as going through trash to find discarded credit card bills. Whatever the method, the results can be devastating for the victims, who may suddenly find that thousands of dollars of unauthorised charges have been made on their credit cards or that their chequeing account has been gutted or that their credit score has plummeted.

Fraudsters are creative. Here are the most common methods now being used to steal someone's identity:

Shoulder Surfing

Many fraudsters simply stand behind victims while they use ATMs to withdraw money or credit cards to make phone calls. A bold thief may also stand close enough to a victim using a phone in a public place to hear him or her providing a credit card and pin number to a business such as a hotel or car rental agency. The thieves remember the information and use it later.

Bin Raiding

Many fraudsters will go through office dumpsters or home trash cans to find bank account and credit card numbers. Once the criminals have found a National Insurance (NI) number, bank account number or credit card number, they can begin using it to access bank or credit card accounts, gaining control of them and assuming the victim's identity.

Mail Intercept

If your mail is delivered in a fashion that would allow others to have ready access to it (an unsecured mail area in a large apartment building or even a privately-operated mail box), fraudsters may be able to intercept bank statements and credit card bills and easily have them redirected to another location. By the time victims realise their mail was stolen and not just lost, the thieves will have had time to establish a new false identity using the information they have acquired.

Property Theft

Someone who steals your wallet or purse or burglarises your home may not only get money and valuables but also information. They can steal National Insurance cards, driver's licences, bank deposit slips and credit cards and use them to commit identity theft. Workers who visit your home to make repairs can easily steal credit cards or other information without being noticed.

ID Theft at the Workplace

Some fraudsters acquire information about their fellow employees at work or from friends who work in retail or government offices and use that information to commit crimes.

Telephone Fraud

Fraudsters may call a victim claiming that the victim has won a prize or is eligible for a major upgrade on one of his or her credit cards. Fraudsters will frequently ask for a National Insurance number, bank account number or credit card number to verify the offer and will then use the information to commit fraud.

Internet Fraud

The Internet has become one of the tools most frequently used by fraudsters to commit their crimes. Identity theft has become so pervasive online in-part because there are so many ways it can be done. The most common of these are:

Phishing

As the name implies, this method involves casting out fraudulent e-mails with the hope of luring in victims. In most cases, phishing involves sending e-mails that appear to have originated from a financial institution and claim that there is some problem with the victim's account. The e-mail may include a form (or a link to an online form) requesting the victim to confirm the account information and return it to the sender. If the victim responds, the fraudster will then use the information to access the victim's accounts. When this technique is used by phone, it is called pre-texting.

Public records

Fraudsters may be able to access personal information from public Websites (most often governmental Websites such as those belonging to a county clerk or county recorder). Or, sometimes fraudsters can pose as prospective employers or landlords and access detailed information from a credit bureau.

Skimming

This is not actually an Internet fraud, but it employs electronic means to steal victims' identities. Thieves use a data storage device in which they swipe your card for an actual purchase and keep the information, or attach the device to an ATM where they can record information from everyone using ATM cards at that location.

Spyware

Thieves may add attachments to fraudulent e-mails. The attachments (often referred to as spyware) contain code to steal account log-ons, passwords and other data, and the code can be activated if the recipient opens the attachment.

E-mail scams

Victims are often defrauded twice in these scams: Once up front when they send money in response to the scam and then again later when the fraudster uses the identification information the victim supplied for additional crimes.

While there are no guarantees your identity will not be stolen at some time, there are specific things you can do, or keep in mind, to lower the possibility of a fraudster getting access to your

How Your Information Gets Stolen 11

personal information. Here are some suggestions for combating fraudsters:

- Handle your mail carefully. Do not send outgoing mail in a non-secure box, such as a communal mail drop at work or in a larger apartment building. Do not let mail sit in your mailbox, and ask the post office to stop your mail if you are going to be away from home for any length of time. Shred all mail that contains identification information (especially bank statements, credit card bills and credit offers).

- Arrange to pick up new cheques at the financial institution.

- Read your bank statements and credit card bills carefully as soon as they arrive. Be aware of the date on which you typically receive each bill and statement.

- Keep your personal information where it cannot be easily stolen. Keep financial and credit information locked up at home and not easily accessible by thieves. Consider acquiring a safe for your home. Small safes are relatively inexpensive and can be an effective deterrent to a home burglar. A small safe can also be hidden out of sight of the burglar.

- Do not carry your National Insurance card with you. Do not carry more bankcards or credit cards than you will need that day.

- Never give out your National Insurance number or any financial information to an unsolicited caller.

- If it sounds too good to be true, it probably is. Do not believe any offer without checking whether it is legitimate. Do not be badgered into giving out information to anybody making unsolicited phone calls to you.

- For maximum safety, do not open an e-mail if you are unsure who sent it to you. Do not open e-mails that have an empty subject line (or have some nonsense subject), and do not open attachments that come with these e-mails. Make sure the people on your e-mail list know you will not open any e-mail that has no subject on it.

- Do not reply to any online offer that you did not request. Read these offers carefully, especially any e-mails that could be phishing. You may be surprised by how many of these offers have misspellings and incorrect grammar. A reputable company, especially a financial institution, would not send out offers with such errors.

- Type URLs directly into your browser or use your bookmarks. If you need to update account information or change a password, visit the business' official Website. Do not enter personal information into a pop-up window.

- Do not use easily discovered information as a password, such as your birthday, your mother's maiden name or the last four digits of your National Insurance number. Set-up passwords that are a minimum of six characters in a combination of letters and numbers and keep these passwords secure.

- Install and maintain virus protection on your home computer. If your high-speed Internet access is on

How Your Information Gets Stolen 13

all the time, use a firewall. Do not store financial information on a computer. Delete all personal information from a computer before it is sold, given away or discarded.

- Carefully read any Website security information before you submit sensitive information. Request a copy of your credit report every year and check it carefully for any signs of possible identity theft.

- Do a wallet or purse check. You may be carrying more personal information than you realise. If you are carrying credit cards you seldom use, leave them in a secure place at home. If you are carrying your Social Security card, remove it from your wallet or purse and leave it at home.

- Be aware of who is around you when you are using an ATM or punching information into a phone in a public place. You should not feel any embarrassment about shielding a keypad or phone pad. If you are uncomfortable with the activities of someone close to you, move to a different location.

- Shred all of your ATM receipts, credit card bills and financial institution statements when you no longer need them.

- At work, ask who has access to your personal information and what procedures the company has in place to secure your information. You will need to give out your National Insurance number to a new employer, but what happens to that information once you provide it varies widely from employer to employer. Make sure your wallet or purse is secure at work when you are not at your work station, and do not leave personal information in plain view at your work station.

- Never give out personal information on the phone or online unless you have initiated the contact. When you fill out an online form, do not provide your National Insurance number. When you buy anything online, carefully review the site's security policies to make sure your information is protected. A secure online site will have an s following http or will have a closed-lock symbol in the lower left corner of the browser screen. Do not give out personal information via e-mail; e-mail is never secure.

- Never give away or sell a computer without scrubbing the hard drive. Do not carry personal identity information on a laptop computer.

- Create passwords and PINs that are a sequence of random numbers and letters. Memorize the information and keep any copies of it in a secure location in your home. Do not carry the numbers with you or write them on your credit cards.

- Copy the fronts and backs of your credit cards and keep the information in a secure location. That way, if your identity is stolen, you will have the information you need to start combating the theft. Do the same for passwords and PINs.

Early Warning Signs

Often the crime has been underway for many months before a victim sees the signs–the unauthorised charges on credit cards, the phone and credit card accounts that have been established without permission, the depleted bank balance.

Many people are far too busy to check carefully all of their telephone bills, bank statements, credit card bills and credit reports. They simply pay the amount due and file the bill away. Thieves count on this laxness, which allows them time to do the most damage with your stolen identity. One of the keys to fighting identity theft and limiting the damage it can cause is to discover the theft as soon as possible.

Fraudsters will often start small and work their way up. In other words, they will do just a little damage at first and see if it is detected. If it is not, they then increase the action until their activities are detected.

Credit cards offer many opportunities for fraudsters, but they also provide early warning signs that you can look for to detect that your identity is being misused.

- Unexpected and unexplained charges suddenly appear on your credit card bill.

- You start receiving bills for credit card accounts you have never opened.

Bank accounts are a preferred target for fraudsters. Financial institutions know this and want their customers to be aware of the early warning signs. The most important ones are unusual withdrawals or purchases that appear on your online statement or monthly bank statement or if you stop receiving bills or bank statements.

If the amount of e-mail spam you receive suddenly spikes, and you are getting offers you would never pursue–such as ones leading you to pornography sites–your e-mail address has been compromised and sold to other unscrupulous online operations.

Here are some ways to detect your identity has been stolen:

- **Review your credit reports.** Review the reports carefully and look for any activity that you did not initiate, especially if there are new credit accounts appearing that you did not open

- **Examine your bank statements and credit card bill.** It is easy to simply pay your credit card bills each month and file your bank statements without paying much attention to them, but these documents may provide early warning that your identify has been stolen. Look over your statements and bills for any unusual activity (including money transfers, withdrawals, and purchases) and contact your bank or credit card company immediately if you believe there has been unauthorised activity on your account. Also, if you have not been receiving these statements and bills on a regular basis, they may have been intercepted by a fraudster.

- **If you use online banking services, check your account history regularly.** Transactions are often posted in 1 to 2 business days, which means that, if you make a thorough review of your account on a regular basis, you may be able to detect a problem much more quickly than if you only looked at your monthly statements.

- **Examine your brokerage reports.** Fraudsters will try to steal from you by getting access to your investment accounts. Read your monthly statements from your investment company carefully. Determine if all the activity on the account was authorised by you, and make sure your brokerage firm has correct, current contact information for you (address, phone number and e-mail address). Investigate any unusual contact from your credit card companies. Fraudsters may be getting access to your information if you receive phone calls indicating you have accepted credit cards you did not apply for or if a collection agency calls you to collect on bills you did not incur.

- **Discover why you are being denied credit or an apartment.** If you are being denied a loan or a new credit card or are being refused an apartment, ask why you were denied. If you thought your credit was good and find that it is not, it is possible that a fraudster has already used your accounts and has either maxed out your line of credit or has opened completely new credit and left unpaid bills in your name.

- **If your home is burglarised, know what has been stolen.** If you have been the victim of a home burglary or other loss of property (losing a wallet or handbag to a pickpocket, or having your hotel room burglarised), you can safely assume the thieves have not only stolen your physical property but also will use any information they have acquired to steal your identity as well.

- **Stay alert to signs that your trash has been ransacked.** If it looks like someone has been going through your trash, do not overlook the fact that the bin raider was likely looking for your identity information as well as for any other possibly valuable items. If you have discarded any bank or credit card information recently, be proactive about notifying your bank or credit card companies that your identity may have been stolen. One way to stymie bin raiders is to shred all sensitive documents (including credit card offers) before you dispose of them.

- **Notice if you are not receiving your normal mail.** You should be aware of when you normally receive phone bills, bank statements and credit card bills in the mail. If it seems you are not receiving any of these on their usual schedule, it is possible that your identity has been stolen and the bills are being redirected elsewhere. Contact your post office if your mail is not being delivered as you would expect. They may be able to explain why the delivery has been disrupted and if they have no explanation, your mail may have been intercepted. While there is little the post office can do to prevent your mail from being stolen by a fraudster, they can help you to at least rule out the possibility that the problem was on their end.

- **Recognise when you are receiving a large number of unsolicited phone calls.** Be especially aware of any collection calls from credit companies or from a collection agencies that you believe were not generated by any of your own transactions.

- **Carefully monitor your e-mail.** Similar to receiving unusual snail mail or phone calls, keep vigilant about the kinds of e-mails you are receiving. Do not open e-mails without a subject line, do not open attachments from anyone you do not recognise (especially if there's nothing in the subject line) and never respond to any requests for your personal information. (Remember, legitimate financial institutions would never send out this type of phishing e-mail.)

It is an unfortunate fact of life that you need to protect yourself against identity theft. As frustrating as this new reality is, it is important to embrace the following ideas:

Responsiveness

Even if you do not think it could happen to you, be prepared to act immediately if you have any reason to believe it has. The problem has to be addressed and will not go away on its own.

Persistence

Recognise the signs of identity theft when you see them. If it looks like something is wrong, check it out. You will need to take the time to find out what has happened to you and to deal with it.

Initiative

Follow up on any indication that your identity has been stolen. Do not assume that law enforcement or your financial institutions will alert you to the theft before you can discover it yourself.

Resourcefulness

You are capable of taking the extra steps to reduce the likelihood that your identity is not stolen by keeping careful track of your identification. Create a backup list of your credit card numbers and phone contact numbers and keep it in a safe place so you can make the necessary calls quickly if your identification is stolen.

Take the time and effort to be vigilant. A few minutes reviewing your bills can save you hours of future headaches. Do not just shrug off any suspicious activity you perceive. Check it out promptly and trust your suspicions. You can limit the damage by reporting any suspicious financial activity immediately. Keep records. Know what charges you have made on your credit accounts and compare them to what you see on the statements.

If you notice a charge that appears to be wrong on a credit card statement, dispute the charge before you pay the bill. That way you can have the disputed amount deducted from your payment. You can then keep that money until you have resolved the dispute. This is preferable for you than disputing the charge after you pay the bill and waiting for a refund from your credit card company.

Review your credit report more than once a year. You can order one free report of your credit report every year by going to _www.annualcreditreport.com.co.uk_. But, reviewing your report once a year may not give you the proper notice you need to promptly respond to identity theft.

Look through your chequebook on a regular basis. A favorite trick of fraudsters is to steal only a few cheques from the back of the chequebook, rather than the entire book. This makes it less likely you will discover the theft until you have gotten to those final cheques.

The Emotional Toll

For many victims of identity theft, the emotional toll the crime takes on their lives is just as serious and real as the financial ramifications. Victims often blame themselves for allowing their identity to be stolen and might find that the steps necessary for recovering from the crime carry an additional emotional toll. Here are some emotional problems commonly associated with identity theft.

Victims of identity theft often feel this crime would not have happened if they had been more vigilant or smarter about guarding their identity. They had always felt they were careful and in control of their lives but now feel that they have made a major mistake that resulted in their identity being stolen.

Victims of identity theft often feel like it will never end, especially when–as sometimes happens–each month they discover an additional fraudulent use of their identity. Victims will have to deal with the crime for many months and will have to do a fair amount of work to stop the bleeding.

Unfortunately, victims of identity theft have to do a tremendous amount of work to inform authorities about the theft as well as inform phone companies, banks, credit card companies and credit bureaus. Undoing the damage caused by identity theft can take between 3 hours and 800 hours of phone calling, letter writing and follow-up.

Identity theft victims may rightly suspect their identity was stolen by a co-worker, family member or friend. This suspicion can, naturally, lead to a feeling that nobody can be trusted, especially with personal information. A victim of identity theft may have trouble trusting anyone in their lives to not victimize them

After awhile, family and friends of identity theft victims may begin to get tired of hearing about the crime and its effects–and they may make this fatigue known. At this point, victims may feel like they are being abandoned by those closest to them. This may also include feelings of embarrassment about the crime itself.

The prolonged process of reporting and dealing with identity theft can make victims feel like they are losing control of their lives. It would be natural to feel powerless for a time if you start receiving collection letters on accounts they did not start or if you are falsely arrested because your identity has been compromised by a fraudster!

It is hard to know which is more difficult: Knowing the fraudster (such as a family member, friend or co-worker) and having to deal with the feelings of betrayal, or not knowing who committed the crime–but always wondering who did it and if it will be done again. Identity theft is perceived as a particularly cowardly crime and the victim often feels that the fraudster is beneath contempt.

The first wound suffered by the victim of identity theft is the discovery of the crime and the realization of the financial affect. The secondary wounding can involve reporting the crime and dealing with the sometimes difficult bureaucratic process of law enforcement and credit agencies.

Victims of identity theft usually react with anger when they realise what has occurred to them. This is certainly understandable, but this anger can interfere with dealing logically with the effects of the crime and solving the problem. After being victimized by identity theft, some people want to shut down and not use bank cards and credit cards or not use the Internet to access financial information or to shop.

A victim of identity theft may not initially believe they could have been victimized. Crimes are things that happen to other people. These feelings of denial can lead to a failure to deal promptly with the actual crime. Sometimes accepting the fact that your identity has been stolen can lead to clinical depression. Victims may not be able to find the energy to deal adequately with the crime.

Some victims of identity theft falsely believe the problem will go away without them having to undergo any unnecessary hassles in their lives. But, this is not true. The problems will not go away by themselves.

The Solutions

Only time will really heal the emotional wounds of being a victim of identity crime. As victims work with law enforcement, their banks and credit card companies to halt the crime, they will usually feel more empowered about the situation, and this can help ease the emotional stress. Beyond that process, here are some ways you can alleviate some of the immediate emotional effects of finding out your identity has been stolen and is being fraudulently used:

Assume that the process will take time. Recovering from identity theft can literally take months. Do not add to the amount of stress you are quite naturally feeling by allowing yourself to become frustrated about how long the process takes.

There is no reason to feel embarrassed. Feeling foolish is not going to solve the problem. Identity theft can happen to the most careful people, and blaming yourself is counterproductive to the healing process.

Go for support. You not only need the assistance of law enforcement officials and those who work on your financial accounts but also the support of those who have been victimized by identity theft.

Stay organised. One good way to deal with the emotional affect of identity theft is to approach The Solutions in a logical and organised manner. Developing and implementing a remedial plan of action can help you get past the anger, frustration and embarrassment associated with the crime.

Stay engaged with your life. Carry on with the other aspects of your life (such as work, family and social obligations) rather than focusing all your attention on the crime. Be nice to yourself, exercise and turn down requests for your time that you cannot fulfill right now.

Do not expect closure. Even if law enforcement finds and convicts the thief of your identity, you may not feel like the crime has ended. This process can go on long after a thief has been put in prison.

Become an activist. Use your experience as a victim of identity theft to help alert others to the possibility of the crime. Consider joining a support group or becoming part of an online bulletin board to share your newly developed awareness of the crime.

Seek professional help. Discard any negative feelings you might have about consulting a therapist and consider seeking help from one to deal with your emotions regarding the crime.

Keep a journal. Keeping careful records of what actions have been taken and the expected responses can help you deal with the effects of the crime. Consider noting down your feelings as part of your records. Writing down these emotions might help you deal with them.

Leave your anger behind. You have every right to feel angry about the crime that was committed against you, but this anger will not help you deal with the authorities that will help you resolve the problems. Stay focused and logical and deal with people in a respectful way. You might be surprised by how much this helps speed up the healing process.

Realise that you are probably your own best advocate. Realise that the authorities have many crimes to deal with, and so you will probably need to do a major part of the work yourself in identifying the nature of the crime and stopping it.

Keep communicating. Do not be afraid to tell your friends and family what you are going through. They may be tired of hearing it, but you need to keep talking to maintain your energy.

Credit Card Companies and Theft Protection

Having a credit card is a necessity for modern life. You need a credit card to rent a car, secure a hotel room, buy airline tickets and, in some cases, prove your identity. There are many companies offering credit cards, and a smart consumer should consider several factors before selecting a card. Certainly, you will consider the credit limit, the interest rate on unpaid balances and the payment policies before you decide to obtain a card.

But, one factor many people do not consider when obtaining a new credit card is what security measures the credit card company has in place and what their procedures are if your credit card number is stolen and misused. Before you obtain a new credit card, you should know what security measures are common for credit cards and what you will have to do if your credit card number is stolen.

You need to be aware of those moments when your credit card is no longer on your person. Skimming has become a major part of stealing credit card account numbers. Skim artists recruit gofers who take on work in a retail or restaurant business. These people are given small electronic devices–known as skimmers–that will steal the credit information.

- The gofers first swipe the credit card through the legitimate credit card reader to complete the transaction.

- After swiping the card through the establishment's scanner, the gofer will then swipe the card through the skimmer.

- The skimmer will record all the information on the credit card, including the account number and the name and address of the user.

- The skimmer is then returned to the skim artist who can download the information and use it for fraudulent credit card transactions.

A credit card company's policies on identity theft should include notifying you whenever the company believes your card is being improperly used. Some credit card companies do not report suspected theft to the consumer but merely have the activity noted on the credit report. By the time the victim sees the report–if he or she ever does request the report–the damage to the credit rating has already been done.

Some credit card companies do not make it easy to talk to a real person when it comes time to report a possible stolen credit card number. You may find yourself spending a long time working your way through a phone tree and answering prompts before you actually talk to someone who can respond to your problem.

Gold and platinum credit cards are the cards of choice for fraudsters. These cards have high credit limits, and the thieves know that, as a result, the bank or credit card company may take longer to notice any unusual activity.

Most damage to a credit card account is done very quickly. The thief will use the stolen card for only a few days and then dispose of it to avoid detection. The thief will then look to steal another card.

Members of the military have to be particularly careful in selecting and using credit cards. This is especially true for any military personnel stationed on foreign lands. These people will rely more on Internet transactions and online methods of monitoring their financial accounts. They must be very sure the online transactions with their credit card companies are secure.

A pre-approved credit card does not mean you will automatically acquire the card if you apply. The pre-approval only means you are approved to apply for the card. You may not receive the card based on your credit history, and the card may be undesirable anyway–it may have a low credit limit or very high interest rates.

Mail thieves may steal your credit card when it is delivered to you, but the card cannot be used by the thief until it is activated. The activation process can pose a stumbling block to the thief, but only if the credit card company requires activation information that is truly secure.

Credit thieves will not only go after your credit cards, but they can use your identity to apply for instant credit from retail stores, even from an automobile dealer. Many stores make it very easy to apply for instant credit–usually involving a contract with very high interest rates–but often they are not particularly careful about screening applicants. The store may run the credit application through a credit bureau electronically in a matter of few minutes, but someone with stolen identity information can often successfully get through that credit check.

Before you apply for a new credit card, carefully read the company's security measures for protecting you against unauthorised use of your card. What is your liability will be if your card number is stolen and you detect unauthorised charges on your account? Credit card companies usually have liability limits between $50 and $100 for the card owner on unauthorised charges.

Another factor to consider when obtaining a new card is how good the card's security measures are in monitoring unusual activity on the account. A credit card company should be watching the activity on the account and contact you if they detect sudden large charges on the account or if the card is being used outside the country.

- How will the credit card company work with you once you have discovered a theft?
- What is the limit on your liability if your credit card is stolen and misused?
- What information does a credit card company need from you to activate the card and check on its activity?
- How closely does the credit card company monitor any unusual activity on the card, and how will they respond to any possible credit fraud?

Keep in mind, your credit card account may be sold by the initial issuer of the credit card to another credit card company. This new company may not have the same security measures in place or have the same liability limits as the original company who issued the card

Find out from a credit card company if they will promptly cancel any unusual activity on your card after you have paid the bill. Some companies take a long period of time to cancel the charges if you have already paid the bill.

To avoid dealing with credit card companies that have weak security measures and to avoid credit theft, you might consider instituting a credit freeze on all your accounts.

Most credit card companies will strive to fight fraudulent credit use, but, as a consumer using credit, you still need to be proactive in discovering if your credit is being misappropriated.

- Check your credit card statements carefully every month, or regularly review your accounts online, to look for signs of unusual activity.
- Review your credit report at least once a year, and perhaps more often, to find any evidence of unauthorised use of your credit accounts.
- Keep an eye on your credit card when it is being used in a store or restaurant. It is especially easy to have your card skimmed at a restaurant because, in most cases, the card is removed briefly from your sight.
- Do not carry more credit cards with you than you need.

The Solutions

If you believe your credit card has been stolen, you may choose to cancel that credit card. Find out from the credit company what policies they have in place for canceling your credit card and giving you a replacement.

After notifying you regarding the theft of your credit card number, a financial institution or credit card company usually has 10 working days to investigate the fraud and will notify you of the results of that investigation within 3 days of the its completion.

Privacy Policies

The only way you can guard against doing a transaction with a company with a loose security policy is to carefully review the policy before completing the transaction. You must be aware of what constitutes an adequate privacy policy and how to avoid doing business with companies that will not treat your personal information carefully.

Most online commerce sites will carry an End User Licence Agreement, or EULA, that appears at the end of the transaction. This information will give you some indication of whether information from your transaction will be sold to other companies that can then use the information to send you e-mail spam, make unsolicited telephone calls or fill your mailbox with junk mail.

At the very least a privacy policy should contain basic information regarding how the company protects the privacy of its customers, such as:

- A statement of the company's commitment to protecting its customer's privacy.
- A citation to whatever legal requirements the company is following to secure information.
- How the company will collect information about you.

- How the company will manage the personal information it has collected from you.

- How your information will be protected from marketers besides the company you are doing business with.

- A guarantee that the company will honor your preferences for security.

- A list of the actions you can take if you believe your personal information has been compromised by using this company.

Be aware that sometimes a privacy policy, either online or provided as a hard copy, can be cleverly worded to allow personal information to be shared.

It may seem illogical, but, in many studies, online banking services were shown to offer better privacy policies than large banks with physical branches. A paper trail left in sight in a financial institution can result in easy identity theft.

Your workplace should also have a written privacy policy in place to control unauthorised acquisition of your personal information. The policy should list what information would be reasonably expected from an employee, what contact information needs to be listed for the employee and how employees are expected to guard personal information acquired from the business's customers.

A good privacy policy should include basic information.

- A list of the organisations with which your information will be shared.
- A list of all the purposes your information may need to be shared.
- A description of the information that will be collected and used.
- A statement indicating that your personal information will not be used except for the purposes identified in the privacy policy.
- A statement that any organisation sharing your information will maintain the same privacy policies as the company your are primarily using.
- An assurance that the company will not sell or rent your information to anybody else.
- An explanation of how the company will keep your information secure.
- A statement that an organisation will give you your personal information if you request it in writing.

However, just because a privacy policy looks legitimate and strict, there is no guarantee it is. Take the time to read privacy policies and EULAs very carefully. Most fraudsters expect that consumers will not read these policies in great detail and are skilled at hiding indications that your transaction could make you vulnerable to spam or downloaded spyware. Look for statements such as "Your information may be used from time to time" or "Your information may be shared with third party entities". Also, take the time to research the company you are considering doing business with before signing off on a privacy policy. Keep in mind that the policy is only as good as the company behind it.

The Solutions

Make it a practise to never do business with any company that is unwilling to supply you with a privacy policy, either online or on paper. If you feel uncomfortable, for any reason, about the privacy policy of a company, including a credit card company or financial institution, ask to have it clarified. If you do not receive the information you need regarding the policy, consider using a different company or institution. A financial institution should only need limited information about your personal identity for specific reasons.

- Information you supply on an application such as your name, phone number, address and National Insurance number.

- Information about your transactions that will be printed on your monthly statement or available to be reviewed online.

- Information about your credit history from one of the major credit reporting bureaus.

Often a privacy policy, especially from a financial institution, will give you preferences about what information can be shared and what cannot. For maximum privacy, consider opting out of all options to share your information.

Be very careful when applying for a mortgage or credit card online and when applying for instant credit. Privacy policies related to these transactions can be quite lax and result in stolen identity.

Even if a financial institution's privacy policy indicates that it will not share your information with a third party, it will still probably share information with affiliates. Depending on the opt-out options of the privacy policy, you may be able to prevent your information from being shared in this manner.

Knowledge is your best weapon in dealing with companies' privacy policies. Make sure you know what the privacy policy is at your place of employment. Only a very few individuals should have access to your identity information and only under certain circumstances.

When you complete an application for an apartment, request a statement of privacy from your potential landlord. Your landlord has the right to, and probably will, gain access to your credit report, but the information about you should not be shared with anybody.

Online Banking

Online banking has become a popular way for people to monitor their financial accounts, pay bills and transfer money from one account to another. Most major financial institutions offer some form of online banking, usually with a wide variety of services.

However, despite the advantages and convenience of online banking, many computer users are reluctant to use online banking. A recent survey conducted by Financial Services Authority (FSA) indicated that 95 percent of online banking users believe security responsibility should lie with the bank and of that number, 77 percent of users will avoid online banking if banks shifted loss liability back onto the consumer. This is due to fears about their financial information being compromised. Most banks use sophisticated security and encryption programmes to deter online identity theft, but there are ways a fraudster can get around these protections to access your information online. You need to be aware of how secure online banking services really are and what you should do to maintain your privacy when you conduct financial transactions online.

You have several options when choosing a financial institution.

- You can choose a traditional brick-and-mortar financial institution that does not offer any type of online services.
- You can bank at a brick-and-click financial institution that has physical locations for you to conduct business as well as online services.
- You can choose a virtual financial institution that has no physical locations but rather conducts all of its business online.

Users of online banking services usually log on to a secure Website using their computer, then enter user IDs and passwords and proceed to make their transactions. Some online banking services will also allow you to access your account from a PDA.

There are many advantages to using online banking services.

- Online banking allows you to access your account information, pay bills automatically, transfer funds from one account to another and apply for credit cards.
- Reviewing your accounts online allows you to see almost immediately if a cheque has cleared through your account. In many cases, you can view a copy of the actual cheque and print it from your computer.
- Online services are available 7 days a week, 24 hours a day.
- Some financial institutions allow you to link the account information to your own financial

management software, such as Quicken or Microsoft's Money. This feature makes it easier for you to manage and monitor your personal finances.

There are also disadvantages to online banking.

- Fraudsters who use phishing techniques can use your online banking habits to try to steal identity information.
- If you inadvertently download malicious spyware, it can monitor your keystrokes when you are conducting online banking transactions and access your financial information.
- If there is an interruption in your ISP service or if the online banking service goes down, you will have to visit your financial institution or an ATM to conduct the transactions you want to do.

The Consumer Protection (Distance Selling) Regulations 2000, which apply to all Member States of the European Economic Area (EEA) protect your online transactions. These laws give you some legal footing to address any unauthorised transactions you detect.

Most online banking is made secure through a process known as encryption. A good encryption system can effectively protect your financial information under most circumstances.

- When you sign on to a financial institution's online transaction page, your browser will establish a secure connection with the institution's server.

- This secure session is established by using a protocol called Secure Sockets Layer (SSL) Encryption. This specific protocol uses an exchange of public and private keys to communicate.

- The keys used for a specific transaction are used only for that session and are known only by your computer browser and the financial institution's server.

- The secure sockets layer and the use of one-time-only keys help ensure that another Website cannot impersonate your financial institution's Website or change any information exchanged between you and the site.

- A secured Website can be identified by the letter s that appears after the http or by a closed lock symbol at one of the corners of the browser window.

Most online banking services offer some form of e-mail contact so that you can report any problems with the service or ask questions about your account. However, sometimes it may take a day or two for a financial institution to respond to an e-mail enquiry.

A check of your online accounts to see if a transaction has posted is governed by the same rules as other financial transactions. If your institution will not post a transaction within a certain business day, you will not see it online. Some institutions' online banking is sophisticated enough to indicate when a transaction is pending but has not posted. Just like when you check your printed monthly statement, you will need to pay attention to the funds available figure to confirm how much money remains in your account and factor in any ATM withdrawals, transactions you made after the last posted entry.

The Solutions

To protect yourself from online fraud:

- Review the privacy policies of your financial institution's online banking services before deciding whether you want to conduct any financial transactions on the Internet. Make sure the institution is using proper encryption and keys to secure the information you are exchanging.

- When you examine the security policy of a financial institution or an End User Licencing Agreement, or EULA, attached to one of its transactions, read it carefully to see if your institution's policy allows it to sell your contact information to third parties. The EULA should allow you to opt out of any sharing of information with other companies, and, in most cases, you should opt out of this policy.

- A secure online banking service is not a guarantee that your personal information cannot be stolen, but the problem is generally not with a fraudster accessing an individual transaction anyway, but rather with phishers posing as representatives of your financial institution and requesting you to confirm sensitive personal information.

- Many financial institutions will use cookies to help track your transactions when you are online. The cookies are placed on your hard drive during the course of your online transaction. In most cases, these cookies will not compromise the security of your computer and personal information. If you are bothered by the use of cookies, most Internet browser programmes offer options for you to avoid or delete these cookies. Be aware that some financial institution Websites will not allow you full access without the use of cookies.

- Only have one browser window open when you are accessing your financial institution's online service. Also, log out of the financial institution's Website as soon as you are finished using it. The Websites of many institutions will automatically log out a user after a certain amount of time, which provides a small degree of protection, but this will not prevent someone from quickly looking at your information before the automatic log-off occurs.

- Make sure you are using the most updated version of your virus protection and spyware protection software to avoid online fraud. If you are using an always-on broadband connection, install firewall software to avoid unauthorised intrusion into your computer.

- Do not exchange any financial information via e-mail. If a financial institution confirms your new user ID and password via e-mail, change them and tell your institution not to confirm this information via e-mail.

- Check your bank statements–both online and hard copies–carefully to make sure there have been no unauthorised transactions made on your accounts.

- If you believe there has been any improper access to your financial accounts through an online service, report it immediately to your financial institution. You should not simply e-mail a concern, but phone the institution and report the problem to a real person. Another excellent source of information regarding online consumer protection laws is available at out-law.com.

Peer-to-Peer (P2P) File Sharing

Online computer users can use Peer-to-Peer (P2P) file sharing to access files from other users and to share their own files with others. This is done by creating an informal network of computers, all operating the same software. While file sharing can be a tremendous asset in getting access to information and downloadable music and videos, it also carries a substantial risk of possible identity theft.

Unlike a local area network, LAN, used at the workplace to network computers, there is little or no security involved in P2P file sharing. There is also no network administrator to monitor activity and notice unusual activity that might be harmful to the members.

All you have to do to start P2P file sharing is to download software–often free and easily accessible–that connects your computer to the network of other computers using the same software. Much of this free software is available only for PCs running the Microsoft Windows operating system; few are available for use by Macintosh computers.

P2P file sharing can allow you access to a wealth of information as well as downloadable music and video files. It may be tempting to use these to acquire information and entertainment without going through normal Internet channels that would require payment.

While P2P file sharing sounds like a tremendous resource, it has very real dangers attached to it. These include allowing other file sharers access to your personal information, inadvertently downloading copyrighted files that could lead to legal action against you and downloading computer viruses or spyware and adware that can create havoc on your computer.

Some P2P file-sharing sites will ask you to pay them for access to the network, but one of the major benefits associated with P2P file sharing is that it is usually free–and many people believe that you should never have to pay for it. Be wary of any P2P site that wants to charge you for its services or uses phrases such as 100 percent legal. No P2P file-sharing site is 100 percent legal. Remember, sharing and downloading of copyrighted files is still an illegal activity. However, some computer experts believe that the paid sites are more reliable than the free ones.

Some scam P2P file-sharing sites will not charge you anything, but give you free software if you provide your e-mail address. Once you do that, they will send you along to a free P2P site–and sell your e-mail address to third-party spammers.

Do not click on advertisements you see on your P2P file-sharing site for any reason. If you see something tempting, take the time to do some research to make sure the advertisement and service is legitimate and then access it directly through your browser bar.

Carefully read the End User Licence Agreement (EULA) that software displays during the installation process. Some scam sites make this information very long, rightly believing that many computer users do not bother to read it. Danger signs to whether these sites include spyware or adware can sometimes be found in this information. Do not install the software if you see wording such as:

- From time-to-time we may make your information available to third parties.

- You agree to allow third-party software to be installed your computer.

To get around the free aspect of P2P file sharing, some scam sites will offer you an upgraded or professional version of the software to enhance the file sharing. These are almost always bogus and will provide you no significant upgraded service.

Most information regarding where to find P2P software is spread by word of mouth or by e-mail. You will rarely find authentic P2P software advertised online, in part because most programmes are free and in part because of its uncertain legal status.

It is still possible that the courts will find P2P file sharing to be illegal. So far no large corporate interest has filed a suit (like the music companies did against illegal music-sharing sites), but it is possible that the next big Internet-related legal battle will focus on P2P file sharing. You may go through the effort of downloading this software–or paying for it–only to find out at some point that you can no longer legally use it.

There are more than 30 different types of P2P file-sharing programmes currently available. Some of the most popular–and free–P2P file-sharing programmes are Kazaa (the most popular P2P file-sharing programme), Grokster and Morpheus. The safest way to avoid P2P file-sharing scams is simply to not participate in P2P file sharing. Get your music downloads from legitimate sites, such as Apple iTunes or the newly-legal Napster.

How Your Information Gets Stolen 49

The free P2P file-sharing programmes are not without their scams. These usually involve including advertisements, whether for other products or P2P upgrades, that will activate spyware or adware. Avoid P2P sites that have fake endorsements from legitimate companies. Few, if any, legitimate companies will endorse the still-questionable use of P2P file sharing.

Some distributors of spyware or adware will get their destructive software on your computer via P2P file-sharing programmes through offers of stolen videos or pirated software. The content does not have the damaging computer code. It is hidden in an installer, licence key generator or patcher that you will need to access the offered video or software. Once you download these pathways, the spyware or adware can invade your computer. Virus writers can easily attach malicious code to a file that looks innocent on a P2P file-sharing network. In 2004, the highly-destructive MyDoom virus was first spread by unknowing users of the Kazaa P2P file-sharing programme.

One of the most annoying aspects of using P2P file-sharing programmes is that they can expose you to unwanted pornography and other videos or games that may be inappropriate for children.

No P2P file-sharing programme will label or give notice of the content of any file. The users name the file when they place it on the network. An innocuously or intriguingly titled file may allow malicious members of the P2P file-sharing network to access your computer files or download spyware or adware on to your computer. As a result, it is potentially dangerous to download any file from a P2P file-sharing programme. And although P2P file-sharing programmes usually advertise filters that seem can block inappropriate content, in reality these filters read only the file's title and description–which is created by another user–not the actual content of the file.

The Solutions

Like many issues in avoiding identity theft, if a P2P file-sharing site is offering services that seem too good to be true, they probably are. If for any reason you think you have inadvertently used a scam P2P file-sharing site, stop using it immediately and stop paying any site that charges you. By this time, your computer may have already been infected by spyware, and you will need to purchase spyware-removal software such as Pest Patrol.

Be very careful when you set-up a P2P file-sharing programme. Make sure you select the proper settings when you install the programme. Buy and install spyware or adware detection programmes and upgrade your virus-detection software before you install any P2P file-sharing programmes. Make sure you close your connection to the P2P file-sharing programme when you are finished using it. Simply closing the programme itself may still allow other users to access your computer. This is especially true if you are using an always-on, high-speed or broadband connection.

Talk to your children about whether they are using P2P file-sharing programmes, the dangers involved and why they may not want to install these programmes. Check the family computer or your children's computers to see if someone has installed any P2P file-sharing programmes. If you do purchase legal digital files, turn down any offers for extra software that would allow others to access your files.

And finally, if you have discovered a scam P2P file-sharing site, alert your Internet provider or major search engines–such as Google or Yahoo.

Voice Over Internet Protocol (VoIP)

Over the last few years many people have been turning to Voice over Internet Protocol (VoIP) providers as a lower-priced alternative to traditional telephone services. These systems have several advantages but also a few significant disadvantages. One of those disadvantages is that, as with many Internet services,

VoIP can be used to steal your personal information in much the same manner as e-mail can be. VoIP is a promising and exciting technology but still has to be approached sensibly and with caution.

VoIP allows you to make phone calls over a computer network such as the Internet. VoIP converts the voice signal from your telephone into a digital signal over the Internet, which is then converted back to a voice signal for the call recipient. This is different than going directly through the Internet for an audio or video conference using a computer microphone and/or camera.

You can make a VoIP call using an ordinary telephone with a special VoIP adaptor or directly from a computer using a regular telephone or hard-wired microphone.

Depending on the VoIP service you select, you may only be able to call other people who use the same service. Other, usually more-expensive, VoIP services allow you to call anyone whether they have the same VoIP or not.

Beyond computer security concerns, there are significant real-world disadvantages to using VoIP rather than a traditional telephone service, including ones with major safety ramifications.

- Your VoIP may not connect directly to emergency 911 services.

- Some VoIP services do not work during power outages.
- Many VoIP services do not offer directory assistance service.

Many identity theft experts believe that VoIP is more susceptible to scams than traditional telephone services due to the service's access to your computer. Some VoIP services inadvertently allow fraudsters to make it appear they are calling from a legitimate telephone number you would recognise on your caller ID. This might allow them to more easily gain access to your private information.

VoIP service may make it possible for fraudsters to monitor more easily or alter phone calls. This is far more difficult to accomplish using traditional telephone services.

Unscrupulous telemarketers can use VoIP to swamp users with unwanted phone calls, a process known as Spam Over Internet Telephony (SPIT).

Many wire-transfer services require users to call from their home telephone as a means of verifying their identities before transfers can occur. This system can be fraudulently by-passed by using a VoIP service. If you are only using a VoIP service, you may not be able to make a wire-transfer by phone. Just as with e-mail, VoIP can allow an access into your computer that will allow it to be attacked by viruses or spyware.

Some VoIP providers can allow you to have more than one phone number, including phone numbers with different area codes.

Depending on your service, you can carry your VoIP with you if you travel with your personal computer and have the service installed on your computer. Remember, you will need Internet access for your VoIP to operate. The prices quoted in some VoIP offers look tempting in part because they do not include the cost of broadband Internet access, which is necessary to utilize the service.

To install a VoIP service, you will need to spend more time than you would need to simply plug in a telephone. In many cases, you will need to purchase and install special software, a microphone and a sound card. Depending on your level of computer skill, this could present a problem. If you are using VoIP with a traditional telephone and an adaptor, you can use it when your computer is not running–but this also means you can receive scam offers or SPIT when you are not using your computer.

Interestingly, companies that offer VoIP services have themselves been victimized by scammers who sell minutes of international calls at wholesale prices, then charge exorbitant fees for the termination of the services. The problem of this victimization–which has actually put some VoIP providers out of business–invariably filters down to the user.

Some fraudsters will use stolen credit card numbers to set-up VoIP accounts. Once the victim realises the theft has occurred and notified the credit card company, the fraudster may have built up substantial bills on the service.

Phishing has increasingly become a problem for VOIP users. Traditional phishing involves e-mails that falsely claim to be from a financial institution that asks victims for sensitive financial information to upgrade or repair their accounts. Wary e-mail users will ignore these offers. But detecting VOIP phishing is harder because the scammer has usually set the caller ID to say it is from the financial institution. The phisher leaves a message for the victim to return the call and supply certain information. The victim may be more likely to believe this scam and return the call. The caller will then be sent to a legitimate sounding but phony phone tree. After a couple of prompts, the victim may be fooled into supplying the information.

VoIP phishing scammers are using the open-source programme asterisk to change a PC into a phone-answering system. Some of these scammers are using the PCs they have infected with a virus to make the Internet calls. Be just as aware of VoIP scams as you would be of any phone or online scam. The advantages of this new technology can sometimes blind victims to the dangers of identity theft through VoIP.

The Solutions

If you receive a phishing phone call from your financial institution, do not reply. Just as in e-mail phishing, financial institutions will rarely call you to ask for this type of sensitive information.

Take some time to check out the phone calls you are receiving. If you think you have received a phishing call, take the time to call your financial institution using the phone number printed in the phone book or on your statement or bill and ask if the request you received is valid.

Alert your financial institution and VoIP provider to any scam you think you have detected. Before you sign on to any VoIP provider, carefully check out how aware they are of VoIP identity theft and what measures they have in place to help prevent it. Be aware that VoIP is not regulated by government agencies. If you are having problems with a provider or think you are being scammed through VoIP, there is little or nothing that governmental authorities can do to help.

Upgrade your virus protection and firewalls; they provide some protection from a VoIP-based invasion of your computer. Consider using a combination of VoIP and cell-phone services for your phone needs. You can provide your cell-phone number to your financial institutions. That way, any calls you receive on your VoIP number that claim to be from financial institutions, you can dismiss as illegitimate.

If someone has illegally gained access to your credit card numbers, immediately notify your VoIP provider. They can then cancel your service and set-up a new account for you using a new credit card number that has not been compromised.

Remember, VoIP can offer many advantages in terms of cost saving, but there are things it cannot do. Do not rely totally on VoIP. You may want to keep a landline on a minimum-service basis or a cell-phone for instances when VoIP cannot be used, such as when there is a power outage, or when you need to call for emergency assistance or want to use directory assistance.

Online Shopping: Is the Internet Safer than Mail?

Shopping by mail and by telephone is slower and less convenient than shopping online. In addition, there is no guarantee that the traditional shopping methods are any safer than using the Internet. Fraudsters can intercept outgoing mail and use the telephone to commit fraud. On the other hand, shopping online can present some of the same challenges as shopping in person, by phone or by mail, including poor service and difficulties with returns.

Shopping online has many advantages. It allows you to do more research and do more product comparisons than you could if you were visiting a store or browsing through a catalog. Also, there is no closing time for online shopping sites. They are open 24 hours a day, every day. And people who live in remote, rural areas and have limited access to shopping malls can especially benefit from shopping online. However, there are also disadvantages. There is often no price advantage to shopping online because you usually have to pay shipping costs in addition to the cost of the product. In addition, shopping in an actual store allows you to see and touch the product before purchasing it–and it also enables you to take it home immediately.

When you shop online your computer will acquire cookies. Cookies can be used by the online retailer to track your browsing patterns and send you advertisements targeted to those patterns. Cookies do not carry viruses and cannot steal information from your hard drive. They usually store information so that your next visit to the shopping site will be customized to your needs.

Often when you shop online you will be asked to fill out a form. This is an area in a Webpage where you will supply specific information on what you are buying, where it will be shipped and how it will be paid for. Forms can be risky because the information you supply in them can be misused.

Many online shopping sites will give you the option to either have or not have your information shared with other companies. You can usually find this information in the site's online privacy policy.

Often you will be asked to create an account the first time you shop at a Website. This account will allow you to expedite your purchase the next time you visit the site. The account will normally require you to create an address and password for future access.

A popular Internet shopping experience is the online auction. The most well-known of these sites is eBay, but there are others. Basically, online auctions offer a site where shoppers can bid on goods, and the person offering the goods eventually sells to the highest bidder. Most auction sites are careful about screening who is placing goods on their sites and responding to claims of fraud, but it is still possible to be defrauded in an online auction or have your personal information misused.

Fraudsters can operate fraudulent online shopping sites that mimic actual retail site, but will not deliver the products that are promised and are there only to gain access to your credit card or financial information.

It is important to be especially careful of online shopping scams during holiday periods. Fraudsters know that people may be less guarded about providing information during stressful gift-buying holidays, such as Christmas, Valentine's Day and Mother's Day. During these seasons of the year you may receive phishing e-mails for must have offers that ask for information that will be used by fraudsters.

The Solutions

There are a number of ways you can protect your identity when shopping online. The most important aspect to not being defrauded or having your identity stolen by an online shopping site is to make sure you are using a secure Website. A secure Website will use encryption technology to scramble your information so only the site can read it and will have symbols on the Webpage indicating it is secure.

- An s displayed after the http (such as https) on the Website address, or
- a closed padlock or unbroken key displayed at the bottom of the page screen.

Shop online with companies you know. Major retailers or service providers are most likely to have proper security for online shopping. Research any company you have not done business with previously. Also, it may be best to stick with online merchants located in the EEU. By doing so, you are protected from fraud and identity theft by the governing laws.

Secure online shopping sites should include a physical address for the business and a telephone number for customer service. You can use this phone number to call to determine the legitimacy of the business before make an online purchase.

Always carefully read the shopping site's privacy and security policies. Any legitimate online shopping site will offer this information. Also, check this disclaimer to see if the shopping site will share your information with any other sites, which could result in getting spam e-mails. Many legitimate online merchants will belong to seal-of-approval programmes that set voluntary security policies. You can find out if an online retailer is really part of one of these programmes by visiting TRUSTe at *www.truste.org*.

Shopping by credit card is the safest way to shop online. If your credit card number is stolen, your damages will be limited. If you use a debit card number or your chequeing account number and these are stolen, it will be much harder to stop and repair the damage caused by fraudsters. Under no circumstances should you give out your National Insurance or passport numbers when you are shopping online.

No legitimate online merchant needs it to process your transaction.

Be aware of what information is required when you fill out a shopping form. The required fields should be marked–usually with an asterisk–and will normally only include the basic information required for a transaction.

- name
- address
- phone number
- e-mail address
- means of payment

Do not give out your password for an online shopping site to anybody else. The passwords should not be something easy for a fraudster to acquire–such as your birthday or your mother's maiden name–but a series of random letters and numbers. Keep this information stored in a secure location.

Consider using only one credit card for shopping online. This will limit the extent a fraudster can cause any damage and allow you to more easily track your shopping transactions.

Always print and save records of your online transactions. You can usually print the confirmation page from the site, and most online merchants will send you an e-mail confirming your order.

And finally, use the online merchant's order form to do your shopping. Do not submit financial information via a separate e-mail to an online shopping site. Fraudsters may send you a fraudulent e-mail regarding a problem with your account and ask you to resubmit your financial data. A legitimate company will not do that.

E-Mail Scams

The trade-off for the convenience of e-mail is dealing with the large number of unwanted spam messages you receive every day. Literally billions of pieces of spam cycle through the Internet every day offering everything from insurance to pharmaceuticals. Most of the offers are legitimate, but probably unwanted, and you may be spending more time than you realise deleting them.

Others are much more malicious. The Internet has become a prime tool for con artists to work their scams. Often the offers are obviously bogus, but sometimes they are much more subtle and designed to prey on people's desires. By responding to these e-mail scams, you may not only lose the money involved in the fraudulent transaction but also deliver aspects of your identification, such as a credit card number or National Insurance number, to someone who will either use it themselves or sell it to a fraudster. You must treat all unsolicited e-mail with a very skeptical eye and be aware of the most common scams in circulation.

The Most e-mail scams will come from names you do not recognise and in some cases are nonsense names generated by a computer. If you open a scam e-mail, in most cases it will look very amateurish and consist only of text, with many spelling and grammar errors.

Many scam e-mails will include a link to a site that may contain spyware or adware. Or, they request that you indicate your interest by returning the required information to the sender. These are both easy ways to gain entrance into your computer through a back door. There are a number of e-mail scams blasted to millions of unsuspecting recipients every day, including:

- **The fake survey scam** is similar to those you get on the phone, claiming you have been selected for a marketing survey and will receive a small reward for participating. However, some of the questions in the survey will ask you to divulge personal information, such as your National Insurance number.

- **The Advance Fee, Spoof Letter or Nigerian scam** (also known as "419 Fraud" so named after the section of the penal code for this crime in Nigeria) is one of the most famous of e-mail scams and has been around for many years. Despite warnings, people are still fooled by it. The fraudster claims to have some connection to the government of Nigeria or other foreign country or a well-known international bank whose money is somehow tied up. They will promise to transfer money into your account if you cover the costs involved in reclaiming the money. They will also ask you for your bank account number. Of course, the money is being stolen, and any information you provide will be used to steal your identity.

- **Work-at-home scams** involve sending out advertisements that guarantee a steady income for very little work while you stay at home. Many times these work-at-home offers involve processing medical claims, stuffing envelopes, assembling craftwork, placing pay-per-use computers in public places and others. What the ads do not tell you is that you may have to work a lot of hours to make very little money and that you may have to pay numerous up-front costs, such as for materials or advertising. Once you begin, often the promoters will not pay for your work, claiming it is not up to standards.

- **Weight loss scams** offer an amazing new pill or other product that will help you lose weight without diet or exercise. These offers take advantage of your hope of finding an easy way to lose weight. But, there are no pills or topical medications that have been proven to help anyone lose weight.

- **Foreign lottery scams** are less common than the others but are still destructive. The spam e-mail claims that a foreign lottery has excellent odds for the players to win and asks you to send money to buy a fake lottery ticket. The message may claim you have already won–although that is highly unlikely if you have never even heard of this lottery–and all you have to do is pay to collect your money or prize. The scammers will keep any money you send them, and they will use your credit card number to make unauthorised charges.

- **Cure-all product scams** claim that some product is a miracle cure for a serious disease. The e-mail will claim that the product is either an amazing scientific breakthrough or a newly discovered ancient remedy. The e-mail may include case histories or testimonials by consumers as to the product's effectiveness. Most serious ailments have to be treated by physicians using prescription medications, and there are no products available via e-mail that can cure impotency, shrink tumors or treat Alzheimer's disease or other serious illnesses.

- **Cheque overpayment scams** target individuals offering goods for sale online, whether on online auctions or through advertisements. The buyer agrees to pay for the product, but at the last minute the buyer will invent some reason why he or she has to write a cheque for more than the agreed amount and ask you to send back the difference when you receive the cheque. Once you deposit the cheque, you will discover it is no good and you will be out the money you returned.

- **Pay-in-advance credit offer scams** tell you that you have been pre-approved for a guaranteed credit card. They may also offer to repair your credit. All you have to do is pay a processing fee that could be several hundred dollars. Remember, a legitimate pre-qualified offer is only telling you that you have been selected to apply for the card. They do not guarantee you will be approved for the card, and they never ask for an up-front fee. In this scam, any money you pay for processing is gone for good.

- **Debt relief scams** are similar to pay-in-advance credit scams. The scammer tells you that you can consolidate all your bills into one small monthly payment without borrowing any more money. You are told that you will no longer be harassed by creditors or at risk of having your home foreclosed and your car repossessed. These offers usually involve your declaring bankruptcy, a step that should only be taken as a last resort and after careful consideration of its long-term consequences. Not only will you have to pay for this advice, but also you will pay the attorney fees and court costs involved in the filing.

- **Investment scheme scams** will promote, via spam e-mail, investments promising a high rate of return for very little upfront investment. Sometimes these offers are quite detailed, but other times they are deliberately vague about what the investment opportunity really is. The con artist will promote his or her connections, access to inside information and a guarantee on the investment. The money you send for the investment will only be pocketed by the scammer, who will operate in one location for a short time and shut down before being detected.

- **Scholarship scams** are perhaps the cruelest of all e-mail scams in that they target students and parents desperate to find the funds for college. The e-mail scam may say the scholarship is guaranteed or unavailable anywhere else. They will ask you to act fast and say they have very loose eligibility requirements. Of course, you have to send them a fee to apply for the scholarship. The money is being stolen, and, instead of getting a scholarship, the student is out money that he or she could have used for tuition.

The Solutions

There are a number of simple steps you can take to protect yourself from malicious e-mails: Never open an e-mail from someone you do not recognise. If you do, do not open any attachment. These attachments can easily download spyware onto your computer that can monitor your activity and steal your identity.

Consider installing a spam filter on your computer. Many ISPs offer spam protection that can be adjusted by you. Be aware, though, that if you have your spam filter at a high setting, it may misread and block legitimate e-mails or not allow you to open e-mails with large, legitimate attachments.

Only share your credit card information as part of transactions that you initiate. Never send out any personal information in response to a spam e-mail. Delete the e-mail immediately.

You should never have to pay for a free gift. If there is some type of processing or handling fee for a free gift, at the very least it is not free, and, at worst, you have just been conned and will receive nothing in return.

Read all e-mail offers very carefully. Con artists design their offers to trigger a knee-jerk reaction from you. If you want to lose weight or are concerned about a physical condition, consult a physician for a treatment plan or necessary prescription. If you are going to invest in the stock market, work with a reputable broker or legitimate do-it-yourself Website. You can avoid being scammed with simple vigilance and healthy skepticism.

Check out any scholarship offer carefully. You can try to go directly to the organisation to verify its legitimacy or check with a local higher-learning institution's financial aid office to see if this offer is real. You should never have to pay a processing fee for a scholarship application. Be sure to tell your student not to send money to a scholarship offer without allowing you to review the offer first.

Phishing

You open your e-mail to discover you have received a message from your financial institution. It is flagged as urgent, and the subject line reads, Immediate

Attention Needed for Your Account. You open the e-mail and read a message telling you that there has been unusual activity on your account. To prevent further activity of this kind or your account being terminated, the e-mail instructs you to fill out a form–either within the e-mail message or provided by means of a link–with your account number and National Insurance number and to return it immediately.

You are a victim of phishing. The e-mail is a fake, and the information you provide will be used by fraudsters to empty out your bank account or make fraudulent charges. Phishing has become one of the most common ways that fraudsters fraudulently acquire your identity. The schemes can range from the laughably crude to the extremely sophisticated, and even the most savvy Internet users can be scammed. Identifying phishing scams and steering clear of them is imperative in protecting your identification.

Phishing has been around since the earliest days of the Internet with the first recorded instance being noted in 1996. Phishing is an appropriate name for a scam that involves casting out e-mails with the purpose of hooking as many victims as possible. Ph was substituted for f because hackers frequently use this substitution. According to the FSA, the number of recorded phishing incidents in 2005 was 312, the figure for the same period in 2006 was 5,059–an 8,000 percent increase!

There is growing evidence that phishers have become more selective. Rather than sending their e-mails indiscriminately to as many users as possible, now many phishers target specific computer users based on knowledge of what credit cards they have and what financial institutions they use. The thief can then send out fraudulent e-mails that look like they are from one of these specific institutions, increasing the likelihood that the victim will assume it is real because it is from a company or institution they use. This method has been termed Spear Phishing.

Often phishing attempts are very crude, with links to Webpages that look obviously fake and with e-mail messages containing misspelled words and grammar mistakes. Credit card companies and financial institutions will never contact you via e-mail requesting your National Insurance number or account numbers, and they would never send messages containing basic spelling and grammar errors.

Phishing e-mails will usually use an introduction line such as Dear Valued Customer. A legitimate e-mail from a credit card company or financial institution will usually use your name in an introductory line.

Most phishing attack e-mails will include threat messages or deadlines to spur you into activity by stating your account will be closed if you do not respond within a certain time frame.

More sophisticated phishers may include an URL to a fake Webpage, and once you have input the requested information and it is logged by the fraudster, the fake page will redirect you to the actual financial institution Webpage, giving the impression that this was a legitimate request. However, the initial link to the fake Webpage can be a giveaway to the phishing attempt.

- The URL will have a subtle misspelling. For example, your bank's real URL may be *www.barclays.co.uk*. The phony URL might say *www.barclay.co.uk*. Typos like this one are easily missed, and the victim may wrongly believe they are going to the actual financial institution.

- The URL will include an @ as part of the address making it look like you are accessing your financial institution, but actually redirecting you to a fraudulent Webpage. For example, you may receive a phishing e-mail with the URL link of *www.barclays@citywide.co.uk*. When you click on that link, you will not reach Barclays Bank as you expect, but rather Citywide, which is a cover name for a phishing scam site.

The Websites used in these scams typically do not contain basic information about the company or financial institution, such as an address or phone number. The phishers do not want to provide any information that will help you verify that the request is fraudulent.

Most phishing attacks take place from Web servers that have been compromised by hackers, often in foreign countries. As a result, it is very difficult to track down where the phishing attack is coming from. Some phishers may link together several compromised servers that they can control remotely. These are referred to as Botnets.

Phishing can also be done over the phone with callers targeting victims and calling them to supposedly alert the victim to a problem with his or her account and requesting verifying information. This type of phishing is called Pre-Texting. But not all calls that sound like pre-texting are pre-texting. Some information about you is a matter of public record, such as whether you own a home, pay your real estate taxes or have filed for bankruptcy. If someone calls for this type of information, they are probably not pre-texting you.

Vigilance while using the Internet is key to avoiding these scams and other attempts at identity theft. Do not reply to any e-mail requesting your personal information unless you initiated the transaction. Even if you do not fill out a form on a fake Webpage, the simple act of clicking on the link and opening that page may open your computer to virus attack or an invasion of spyware or adware. Avoid clicking on the link and do not cut and paste the link into your Web browser. In general, you should never open an attachment or use a link included in an e-mail from anyone you do not recognise.

The Solutions

Never enter any personal or financial information into a pop-up window. Phishers can use pop-ups to attach bogus requests onto legitimate Webpages. The phishers' plan is that the victim will think that the pop-up is a legitimate request for information.

Keeping your anti-virus software up to date will not stop all phishing attempts or e-mail scams but will prevent many of them. These programmes are constantly being upgraded to respond to the latest innovations by clever fraudsters. If you are using a high-speed broadband connection that is always on, install firewalls to help block phishing attempts.

If you think you have been caught by a phisher, check your next credit card bill and bank statement to see if there has been any unusual activity on the account. Use a phone number you know is correct and contact your institution to check whether there is a problem. You can also contact the institution via its correct Website. As with other attempts at identity theft, request a copy of your credit report and examine it carefully. Also, change your passwords immediately if you think you have been conned into giving out this information to a phisher.

Be proactive if you think you have been phished. Taking the following steps may help prevent others from being victimized, too!

- Alert the company that supposedly sent the fraudulent e-mail to what you have received. Forward the actual e-mail to them along with any additional information you can provide.
- Report phishing e-mail to the Anti-Phishing Working Group—a combination of ISPs, law enforcement agencies, financial institutions and software security vendors who are trying to fight phishing at *www.reportphishing@antiphishing.org*.

Contact CIFAS to earmark your name and add with 'protective registration' so that anyone applying for credit in your name will automatically be double-chequed and additional proof of identification will be required.

More information is available at these Websites:

Anti-Phishing Working Group, *www.antiphishing.org*;

International consumer Protection Enforcement Network, *www.icpen.org*;

Identity Theft Secrets, *www.identitytheftsecrets.com*.

Spyware and Adware

Every time you use the Internet you open a door into your computer that hackers can use to sneak uninvited software into your system. In some cases, this software is relatively benign, if still annoying. This type of software is generally called Adware. However, a more insidious type of unwanted software can track your Internet use and access your personal information without your knowledge. This type of software is called Spyware. It is important that you be aware about what these types of software can do to your computer and your identity and how to prevent receiving this unwanted software.

Adware is usually not meant for truly malicious purposes. In its more benign forms it can simply lead to annoying pop-up ads appearing on your browser. Adware can also profile your online surfing and spending habits but generally will not go after your identification. At the very least, accidentally downloading adware can lead to a lot of annoying time in clicking out of unwanted ads. At the worst, it can cause your computer to slow down or even lock up.

In most cases adware is a legitimate source of revenue for companies who offer their software for a limited time as freeware. The adware shows up in the form of pop-up windows while you are using the freeware.

Some adware is engineered to overwrite affiliate tracking links. Those links are used by legitimate Webmasters to sell products and fund their sites. This adware is called Parasiteware. Although its use is frustrating for the Website operators, it does not hold much threat for the end user.

Spyware is also known as Snoopware, PC Surveillance, Key Logger, System Recorders, Parental Control Software, PC Recorder, Detective Software and Internet Monitoring Software. In general, it is referred to as a Trojan horse programme, because it can enter your computer hidden within software you wanted. Spyware is not in and of itself against the law, but some of its uses are.

Spyware is the more dangerous of the two types of software you might accidentally download. Spyware goes beyond annoying you with ads. It records your keystrokes, surfing history, passwords and other identification information.

Both adware and spyware can enter your computer by being bundled into other software, frequently free software referred to as freeware. This freeware might be a free e-mail programme or a computer game. Once you download the software you want, the bundled adware or spyware is activated onto your computer and begins doing its work. A clue to whether you are downloading unwanted adware or spyware will be found in the End User's Licence Agreement, or EULA. The information there will refer to the freeware usage including other software to be downloaded on your computer.

Adware and spyware can also be downloaded in a manner called Drive-by Downloading. This method downloads the unwanted software by using misleading dialogue boxes during the download.

Using P2P file-sharing programmes–in which users belong to an informal network linking them to other users–is an excellent way to spread adware and spyware. Many P2P users are younger computer users who are not aware of what they are passing along or acquiring from other computers.

Some computer users deliberately download spyware as a way to monitor what their spouses or children are doing on the computer. The danger, of course, is that this spyware is doing much more than spying on computer usage for the operator. It is stealing identification information at the same time.

Beyond spyware, which carries with it the potential for identity theft, there are other, even more dangerous versions of software that can attack your computer.

- Malware is slang for malicious software that is specifically designed to disrupt your computer system.

- Page Hijackers are applications that try to take over your home page and substitute it with one of their choosing.

- Dialers are used by pornographic vendors. This software disconnects you from your modem's usual ISP and moves the service to another phone number. You still get billed from your ISP. This software will not spy on you, but it can potentially cost you a lot of money.

Due to the fluid nature of the technology and the cleverness of the spyware creators, it has been difficult to even establish any case law to combat the problem. Some corporations have sued identifiable creators of software and adware because of the damage caused to their businesses and loss of productivity.

The Solutions

One of the keys to combating spyware and adware is, first, identifying that you have downloaded them. This is not easy, but it is possible. Take a good look at your Web browser and see if some of the settings have changed. Those changes could include extra toolbars, new home page settings and changes to your security settings or favorites list.

You may detect a spyware infection when you see pop-ups appear that have absolutely nothing to do with the site you are visiting. Most legitimate pop-ups will have some relationship to the site. Often adware or spyware appear in unsolicited ads for pornography and are not displayed in the way you would see other, more typical, ads.

If you click on a hyperlink that does not work or takes you someplace you did not expect to go or if your computer noticeably slows down in operation, then your system has probably been infected by adware or spyware.

Like virus protection programmes and firewalls, there are programmes available for blocking and removing spyware. Some of these are more effective than others, and, no matter how they are advertised, none of them are 100 percent effective in blocking all unwanted software. However, it is still useful to install one of these programmes. Just do your research to find out which ones are the most effective. Be aware that some programmers have developed bogus anti-spyware software that is advertised in banner ads on a Webpage. In some cases, these programmes will not only not work but will actually add more spyware to your computer.

One of the best ways to prevent the inadvertent loading of adware or spyware is to carefully read the EULA of any software you download online.

Programmers who bundle adware or spyware onto other software, such as Freeware, know that most people will not read a long EULA. They will also couch the existence of the unwanted software in obscure language that less-sophisticated users will not catch.

Make sure your family members are aware of the dangers of adware and spyware and that they are all careful about what they download. Discourage all family members from using P2P programmes.

Do not make the mistake of automatically downloading a tempting freeware programme as soon as you see it advertised or hear about it from friends or family. Take the time to take a look at who is offering the freeware and be aware of the possibility that unwanted software may be bundled into it. In general, legitimate software providers will not bundle in unwanted software. Lesser-known game programmes, e-mail and pornography are the usual carriers of unwanted software.

If you operate a business, create and enforce a policy against downloading any software from the Internet. All software should be either downloaded by you or the system administrator or purchased as a CD and loaded as needed. Adware and spyware can not only damage your computer system but also create a serious loss of productivity from employees who have to click out of pop-up ads.

For additional information about Adware, Freeware and Spyware visit:

Spyware Guide, *www.spywareguide.com*,

FaceTime Communications, *www.facetime.com*,

Adware Info, *www.adware.info*.

New Threats to Online Security

The ingenuity of online fraudsters continues to grow and will likely do so for the foreseeable future. In a seemingly endless cycle, as soon as anti-virus, firewall and anti-spyware software are modified to deter hackers, the hackers come up with new ways to gain access to your personal information.

Although there are some well-established rules to follow to improve your online security – not responding to phishing scams, avoiding file sharing and not opening any suspicious e-mails or attachments–you also need to keep abreast of developments in the online security arena so you can incorporate new tips into your security routine as soon as you hear about them. It may seem daunting, but the new steps may be as simple as purchasing new software or slightly modifying your online activities to avoid being victimized by the latest in online identity theft.

Once the domain of only the most sophisticated hackers, botnets are now quite commonly used to hijack personal computers and then use those computers to send out spam viruses or Internet attacks on vulnerable servers. In some cases, criminals are purchasing botnet kits to implement their crimes. The bots allow hackers to use simple command-and-control signals to send their scams through another computer or network.

One place that potential criminals can go for botnets is a Website called Metaphisher. According to iDefense Labs, a company that provides security consulting services to governments and corporations, this one downloadable product has infected more than one million personal computers around the world. The botnet relays almost every type of information from the computer to the hacker, including the computer's location, what security patches are installed and all the browsers installed on the computer. Under most circumstances, the process of using these botnets for malicious purposes is relatively easy.

- The hacker buys a botnet kit online for a nominal fee and then builds a bot not yet known to antivirus suppliers. This is a relatively simple process.

- The bot is sent out as an e-mail attachment or is placed on malicious Websites.

- The botnet then can generate income for the hacker by distributing spam, spyware and denial-of-service attacks.

File transfer protocol or FTP Websites are designed to allow computers to share information. However, they are increasingly becoming targets and tools of fraudsters who access personal information posted on FTP sites. Often fraudsters will deposit personal information they have acquired onto an open FTP site; that personal information can then be accessed by anyone who stumbles across the site. Online security companies such as Sunbelt Software has found so many of these data resource sites, they have stopped contacting the individuals involved and are simply turning the reports over to authorities to investigate.

Fraudsters using the Internet recently set-up an eBay auction trap to access personal information. The phishers found a vulnerable part of the eBay site and were able to add fake auction links to the site. The links, when followed, asked for the user's eBay log-in information, which could then be used fraudulently. The fraudsters correctly reasoned that many people would not supply this information from a phishing e-mail but would do so if the link was part of a Website that they knew and trusted.

Domain name servers are vital to Internet usage. They allow you to type in a user-friendly Internet name–such as www.xyz.co.uk–into your Internet address bar; your computer then translates the user-friendly name into the series of numbers and letters used to actually access the site. Cybercriminals can misconfigure these names to direct users to a fraudulent Website. It is believed by Internet security experts that almost 75 percent of Domain Name Servers are running old or misconfigured software, making it easy for a hacker to target everyone on the Domain Name Server and send out an e-mail that looks as though it is coming from a legitimate site. If you were one of the victims of this scam, the next time you type in an address, such as www.yahoo.com (the correct address is *www.uk.yahoo.com*), you would be directed to a Website that would download a variety of malicious software to your computer.

Rootkits are becoming increasingly popular for hackers distributing malware. The rootkits effectively hide viruses, worms, bots and other malicious software without being detected by anti-virus software. The rootkits operate in three basic steps.

- The rootkit invades your computer through a Trojan horse, either at a malicious Website or by means of misleading dialogue boxes during a download (also called drive-by downloading).

- Once the rootkit has gained access, it downloads malware that can make significant changes in the computer's deep system to avoid being detected by anti-virus software.

- The Trojan horse, now camouflaged, can install keystroke loggers and spyware onto your computer.

Viruses cannot only attack your computer but also lately have been used to go after cell phones. Some can destroy the cell phone's operating system; others are merely nuisances.

Users of non-Windows-based computers such as Macs or computers running Linux have believed they were much safer from virus or spyware attacks. Although this may have been true for a time, this may no longer be the case. The Mac Operating System X, or OSX, has 70 reported security holes that are being used by criminals, and the number of malicious programmes targeting Linux doubled between 2004 and 2005. In addition, some viruses and spyware are now being designed to be cross-platformed, meaning they can infect a variety of computer operating systems.

The new computer attacks not only target personal computer users but also companies using local area networks or LANs. IT professionals are constantly fighting off computer attacks.

- The odds are one in six that a company will have a laptop or PDA stolen or misappropriated.
- The odds are four in five that companies store data files that are unencrypted.
- The odds are two in three that transfer data files are unencrypted.
- The odds are one in two that a company limits employees from downloading software onto their computers.

- The odds are one in five that a company will suffer network or data sabotage.

- The odds are one in four that a company will not know if its computers have been illegally accessed.

- The odds are two in five that a company does not keep a log of computer security incidents.

- The odds are nine in ten that a company suffered a computer security incident during the past year.

The Solutions

Botnets, like most other types of malware, cannot infect your computer unless you open the wrong e-mail or e-mail attachment. You should never click on any attachments or links in an unsolicited e-mail.

Internet Explorer, one of the most common Web browsers in use, is the biggest target of those distributing botnets and other malicious software. Consider using a different type of browser, such as Firefox, Opera or Safari, which are targeted less.

To combat having your information taken into an FTP site, install a firewall that can block unknown programmes from communicating with the Internet. The firewall installed with Windows XP or Vista will not do this. However, others–including the free ZoneAlarm firewall–will allow you to block this access.

Using unique passwords for different Websites and frequently changing passwords will help prevent your information from being usable through a FTP Website.

It is up to you to remain vigilant about the latest online threats to your privacy. It is important that you keep up with all available information–in magazine articles, in books and on the Internet. For the latest updates you might want to visit F-Secure at *www.f-secure.co.uk*, Kaspersky at *www.kapersky.co.uk* and Sophos at *www.sophos.co.uk*.

Make sure your ISP is using a domain name server that is running up-to-date software, and consider checking with the ISP on a regular basis to make sure it is staying on top of any potential problems.

Rootkit scanning is difficult and has been compared to shining a flashlight into a dark room and trying to identify the objects by the shadows they cast. There is software that will scan for rootkit entry into your computer, but as of yet none of these are 100 percent effective.

Even though virus infection of cell phones is not a major problem yet, odd are good that this problem, too, will grow. You should disable open Bluetooth on your cell phone or PDA to block the most-used route to infect the phone, and monitor your cell phone bills for unexpected charges. You can also install cell phone anti-virus programmes, similar to those on your computer.

If you are using a Mac or a computer running Linux, you should consider using antivirus software designed for these systems, such as Panda Antivirus for Linux and McAfee and Symantec for the Mac. Whatever your operating system, make sure your security is up to date and all your patches are current.

Part 2

DIFFERENT FORMS OF THEFT

While individual identity theft is the most common form of identity theft but there are other less common forms you should be aware of to avoid becoming a victim. In this chapter we will review each type of theft and the steps you can take to protect your valuable information:

- Individual identity
- Financial, account takeover and new account set-up
- National Insurance number
- Business identity
- Bankruptcy and fraud
- Theft of your children's information
- Mortgage Fraud

Individual Identity

Identity theft is a broad term that refers to a wide variety of crimes, but at its essence identity theft is just what it sounds like:

Appropriating information about you that can be used to establish a false identity using your name and other forms of your identity.

Once this false identity is established, a resourceful thief can then pose as you for a variety of fraudulent purposes: To empty your bank accounts, open new credit card accounts, purchase cell phone services or modify your existing phone service and even misuse your Internet Service Provider (or ISP) for fraudulent Internet transactions. You must know how your identity can be stolen and misused and the general signs that this has occurred in before you can recognise that the theft has occurred to you.

Most people carry their identity with them: They carry credit cards, debit or ATM cards, driver's licences and National Insurance cards with them everywhere they go. A thief can steal this information by simply picking a pocket or stealing a purse.

An essential part of your identity is your National Insurance number. Although this number was not created to be a form of universal identification, it has become so over the last 90 years. You may be asked to supply your National Insurance number for transactions that do not really require you to provide it.

Most fraudsters work in teams. One member of the team will steal a wallet or purse and hand it off to his or her fellow criminals in a nearby vehicle. By using simple technology–such as a scanner, PC and laminator–the team can create a new, fraudulent form of identity in just minutes.

Once a fraudster has access to your identity, there are many ways the information can be misused. The thief can:

- Set-up new phone accounts in your name.
- Establish new credit card accounts in your name.
- Access your financial accounts.
- Access your ISP and make Internet transactions in your name.
- Create new forms of identity, such as a driver's licence, in your name.
- Gain access to your credit reports and misappropriate the information that appears on them.

Often, identity theft can occur when friends or relatives visit your home. It is not unusual for people who are experiencing credit difficulties to steal the identity of a friend or relative–even a child–in an attempt to start their lives over by establishing new credit.

Many people are very careless about how they store their personal information at home.

- They leave chequebooks in clear sight and within easy access.
- They do not hide credit card bills or application forms.
- They do not secure their National Insurance numbers or passports.

Your workplace can also be a place of access for fraudsters. Your personal information, including your National Insurance number, will usually be on record at your workplace. While you may not want to believe it, it is certainly likely that your personal information could be accessed and stolen by a fellow employee.

Although Internet-based identity theft is less likely to victimize you than actually having your identity stolen by a pickpocket or purse snatcher, fraudsters still try to use the Internet for identity theft by sending out phishing e-mails–bogus requests to verify personal information for a credit card account, ISP or financial institution–or by sending out spyware that can track your computer usage.

The Internet is not the only technology that a fraudster can use to acquire your personal information. Sophisticated thieves will use a technique called pre-texting. Pre-texters will call you and try to extract personal information from you in a similar fashion as phishing.

Much identity theft takes place through the mail. Fraudsters go through your trash to find credit card bills or financial statements. Or, your mail may be intercepted before you receive it–and before you have a chance of realizing that you are not getting the mail you normally expect.

While identity fraud is certainly a concern, there are other facts to consider before overreacting to the possibility of identity theft. The Better Business Bureau conducted a study in 2006 that revealed some interesting statistics.

- The number of identity theft victims has almost doubled between 2003 and 2006, from 46,000 people to 80,000 people in the UK.
- Although the number of victims has decreased, the fraud amount costs the economy $1.5 billion.
- Sixty-eight percent of identity theft victims do not incur any out-of-pocket expenses.
- The time involved to resolve identity theft issues has increased from an average of 33 hours in 2003 to 48 hours in 2006 and may involve contacting 20 to 30 different organisations.

- Most identity theft–90 percent–takes place through physical theft and not via the Internet.
- Young adults are more likely to be victims of identity theft than older adults.

Your identity is not only a matter of finances and credit but is an intensely personal part of you. A victim of identity theft is likely to feel just as much emotional impact from identity theft as financial impact.

The Solutions

One of the most important pieces of information fraudsters want to steal is your National Insurance number. You should do everything you can to keep your National Insurance number protected.

- Do not carry your National Insurance card with you.
- Do not leave you National Insurance card in plain sight at your home.
- Do not automatically enter your National Insurance number on a form unless you believe it is absolutely necessary. There is no good reason why a doctor or dentist needs your National Insurance number.
- Never give out your National Insurance number online or over the phone unless it is part of a transaction you have initiated. You should never put your National Insurance number into an e-mail.
- Do not include your National Insurance number on your cheques.

Most people carry too much identity information with them. Just because you have six credit cards does not mean that you need to carry all of them with you. Consider only carrying only the one or two credit cards you may need for daily transactions.

Shred your trash. Do not discard credit card bills, financial statements or credit applications intact.

While there is no need to be paranoid in your daily activities, you need to be aware that a fraudster may not be some unknown bad guy. The thief may be a co-worker or family member, and so you must be careful in keeping your identity information from prying eyes, no matter who they belong to.

Be aware of the very real possibility of identity theft while you are travelling. Use traveler's cheques, limit the forms of identity you carry with you and be careful about how you keep you-r information safe while you are in a hotel.

Be aware of shoulder surfers who will attempt to steal your identity by watching you enter an ATM number or punch in credit card information on a public phone. Keep your transactions guarded and be prepared to go to a different location if you detect suspicious activity nearby you.

Keep your emotions in check if you discover your identity is stolen. This type of crime can be especially intrusive and distressing. But remember, identity theft can happen to anyone under any circumstances, and you need to focus on correcting the problem. It will take time, but you can resolve the problem. If you are vigilant in monitoring your credit reports and bills and report credit theft promptly, the theft will likely cease. Most fraudsters will only appropriate your identity for a short amount of time, and, when they believe they have been detected, they will stop misusing your information and victimize someone else.

Financial, Account Takeover, New Account Set-Up

Losing your financial information can result in two types of problems–your existing accounts being used fraudulently and new accounts being set-up in your name. As you guard yourself against forms of identity theft, you must be especially vigilant about your financial information and know what will indicate that your financial information is being misused.

While it is certainly possible your information can be stolen online, it is far more likely that a fraudster will acquire your information in a less high-tech manner.

- Your wallet or purse will be stolen and may contain cheques or your ATM/debit card.

Different Forms of Theft 99

- Your financial information will be stolen from your trash.
- Your financial information will be intercepted from your mail.

However, online theft of your financial identity is still something to be concerned about.

- Fraudsters will send out phishing e-mails that appear to be from your financial institution, asking you to confirm your personal information.
- You can inadvertently download spyware that can monitor the keystrokes on your computer, allowing a thief to learn your user IDs and passwords to grain access to your financial accounts.

It is not your name, but your digits, that fraudsters need to access your financial accounts and possibly set-up new accounts in your name. Thieves need to know your account numbers, user IDs, passwords and PINs to access your financial accounts.

If your credit card numbers are stolen, the credit card company will usually limit your liability to between $50 and $100. If your financial account numbers are stolen, there is really no limit to the damage that can be done.

It is not just the aspect of stealing from your current accounts that can affect you if your financial identity is misappropriated. A thief with access to your financial information can also set-up fake accounts in your name. The thief can then write cheques on these accounts. You will be the one who will have to make these rubber cheques good–or prove that the account was not set-up by you.

Another unpleasant aspect to financial fraud is that thieves can use the information to apply for loans that will never be repaid and will have a negative effect on your credit report. These could include loans for business or personal use, student loans, mortgages, and automobile purchase loans or lease agreements.

Fraudsters will also contact you over the phone and represent themselves as being from your financial institution, saying that they need you to confirm your information. This is called pre-texting. They may be sophisticated enough to give you a return phone number that will connect you to a phony, but official-sounding, phone tree.

Your financial institution will usually mail you a box of new cheques, but if you request it–and you should–they can usually hold them at one of their locations so that you can pick them up in person.

Unsecured financial information in your home is vulnerable to theft and usually by visitors you know rather than by strangers who burglarize your home. It has been estimated that more than half of all fraudsters are friends, family and domestic employees.

Many people store personal financial information on their personal computers or their computers at work. Frequently, this information will include a user ID or password that the user has asked the computer to remember. A thief who steals the personal computer or who looks at a co-worker's computer at the office might easily be able to access this information. The same thing applies to any information stored on a Palm Pilot, or PDA.

Clear signs that your financial identity has been compromised include that you cannot open new chequeing accounts or that your cheques are being rejected by a merchant. The refusal by the merchant is because a thief is misusing the magnetic information character recognition code (or MICR), the identification numbers at the bottom of your cheque, or other information that will appear on your cheques.

The Solutions

Consider using online banking services to monitor your financial accounts. By the time you receive a hard-copy statement, your accounts may have already been compromised for several weeks. The online services of most banks use encryption that makes them very secure.

Never reply to phishing e-mails or pre-texting phone calls. Your financial institution will never try to contact you in this manner. If you think the request is possibly legitimate, contact the institution using a phone number or Website address that you know is real. Do not send any personal financial information via e-mail.

Never write your PIN on your ATM card. Do not place your National Insurance number or a credit card number on your cheque. Cover the keypad when you are making an ATM transaction. Most retail stores will no longer accept cards with Ask for ID written in the signature box.

Also report any lost ATM or debit cards immediately. Phone your financial institution immediately to report the loss and follow that up with a confirming letter. Send the letter by certified mail so that you will have a receipt proving the letter was received by your financial institution.

If you believe your financial account has been compromised, stop payment on all cheques and close the account immediately. You may want to consider opening new accounts in a different financial institution. Report the crime to the cheque reporting service your financial institution uses. You can request that the cheque notification service tell retailers who use their databases not to accept your cheques.

National Insurance Number

Your National Insurance number is a very important part of your identity. You are frequently asked to supply it when you are applying for a job, signing a lease for an apartment, taking out a loan or even going to the doctor. You may be asked for it so often that you do not even think about it any more. But, a stolen National Insurance number can allow a fraudster tremendous opportunity to do many things, from establishing credit cards in your name to gaining access to information from your financial institutions. It is essential to know how a thief can acquire your National Insurance number and what you can do to remedy the situation if you believe it has occurred.

A National Insurance number is not just something adults have. Although it is required from age 16 and up children of all ages may have a National Insurance number that was applied for and granted as early as the date of their birth. Children's National Insurance numbers are just as vulnerable to theft as adults', and a National Insurance number can be used for fraudulent purposes no matter what the age of the person whose number it is.

Applied for through the Department for Work and Pensions (DWP), the DWP will never give out your number to anybody. However, sometimes National Insurance numbers can be acquired through perfectly legal means. If your National Insurance number is part of a public record, such as court and property documents, it can be reviewed by anybody at any time. Some of these records are readily available online. These numbers are sometimes legally acquired and then sold to fraudsters, in some cases through Internet auctions.

However, there are many other ways a fraudster can fraudulently acquire your National Insurance number.

- A thief can simply steal your wallet or handbag or find your National Insurance number in a burglary of your home.

- By stealing your mail and chequeing bank statements or credit card bills, a thief can easily get your National Insurance number.

- Your National Insurance number can be stolen when you provide information to an insecure Website.

- Co-workers can steal your National Insurance number from your personnel records at work.

- Dumpster diver thieves can acquire your National Insurance number from trash you have thrown away without shredding.

- Phishers and pre-texters will try to get your National Insurance number by pretending to be representatives of your credit card companies or financial institutions and asking you to resubmit your National Insurance number.

- Your National Insurance number may be stolen by a thief who pays a person processing information about you to steal your identity.

If the problem of someone fraudulently using your National Insurance number persists, it may be possible to get a new National Insurance number, but that will not guarantee your problem will be solved. The thief will still be able to use your old National Insurance number even if you have acquired a new National Insurance number. The pros and cons to obtaining a new National Insurance card is discussed in length in the chapter entitled *The Good & Bad of Changing Your National Insurance number.*

A relatively recent and sophisticated scam to acquire fraudulently National Insurance numbers is a new phishing e-mail. In this latest scam, the e-mail appears to be sent directly from the DWP or HRMC and will contain a subject line that says Dear National Insurance number and Card Owner. Like many other kinds of phishing e-mails, the message states that your National Insurance number has been illegally acquired and is being misused. It then directs you to a Website that looks as though it is the official DWP Website. The message instructs you to resubmit your National Insurance number. Under no circumstances will the DWP or HRMC ask for this information either online or over the phone.

A stolen National Insurance number can be used for more than just stealing your identity for the purposes of opening credit card accounts or gaining access to your financial information. A stolen National Insurance number could also be used by illegal immigrants to acquire fraudulently a driver's licence or by terrorists to create fake identities that would allow them to operate in the United Kingdom.

A stolen National Insurance number, in some cases, can also be used to file a fraudulent tax claim. You may suddenly be notified by the HM Revenue & Customs (HMRC) that you owe taxes that you really do not.

Your National Insurance number may be used fraudulently by people applying for a job or for an apartment or flat. Sometimes these fraudsters either have a problematic credit or employment history that their real National Insurance number would reveal or they do not have a National Insurance number of their own at all. By using your National Insurance number, they can avoid the red flags that would appear if they were honest in their application for a job or an apartment.

Many businesses may request your National Insurance number, usually for their own marketing purposes, but very few can actually demand it. The most common required requests for your National Insurance number will be from state motor vehicle departments, tax agencies, welfare agencies and other transactions requiring tax information such as banks, brokers, potential employers and landlords. You can legally refuse to give your National Insurance number to anybody who cannot demand the information.

The Solutions

Do not provide your National Insurance (NI) number just because you are asked for it. There is really no reason why a doctor's office or small business needs your National Insurance number. If they will not serve you without it, find someone who will.

Keep your NI card at home in a secure location. Do not carry it with you in your wallet or handbag, making it easy for thieves to steal it from you.

Never use any portion of your NI number as a user name or password. You may be tempted to use the last four digits of your NI number as a password because you can easily remember it, but even that can provide information that might be misappropriated.

Do not have your National Insurance number printed on your cheques, driver's licence or any other miscellaneous financial information.

Instead of providing your National Insurance number on a job application, consider telling a potential employer you are willing to provide your National Insurance number as part of a job interview.

If you think your National Insurance number has been fraudulently acquired, do not expect the DWP or Home Office to fix problems related to the theft of your National Insurance number. There is nothing they can do about fixing your credit or financial status. You will still have to work with your financial institutions and credit card companies to correct the identity theft problem.

If you think someone is fraudulently using your National Insurance number for work purposes, report your suspicions to the Department for Work and Pensions and contact CIFAS immediately.

As in many cases of identity theft, the best ways to discover if your identity is being misused is to carefully review your credit card bills and financial institution statements and periodically request and review your credit report.

Business Identity Theft

Consumers are not the only victims of identity theft. Larger companies with extensive IT departments have taken steps to prevent identity theft, some more effective than others. Unfortunately, smaller businesses and retailers–which most people deal with more often than large corporations–are more likely to have their identities stolen. Consumers must realise that companies are just as vulnerable to identity theft as individuals are and be aware of this possibility when providing personal information to businesses.

Most businesses operate with a Business Identification Number, for invoicing, taxes and other internal uses. This number is similar to a National Insurance number in that it is unique to the individual business. Frequently, sole proprietor business operators use their National Insurance number to serve as their Business Identification Number. Either way, business fraudsters may target this number to open bank accounts or send out fraudulent invoices.

Some businesses have been receiving faxes that appear to be from HM Revenue & Customs (HRMC). The fax identifies the business owner as a non-resident alien and requests that the owner fax personal and financial information back to the HRMC on a fake such as: *Form W-8BEN-11* to protect the owner's exemption from specific taxes. The form may request the victim's passport information, National Insurance number, mother's maiden name, financial account numbers and other personal information

One of the most popular business scams can also be a way to acquire business identification information. Those are the Toner Phoners. These are fraudsters who call businesses with supposedly great deals on toner for computer printers or copying machines. At the very least, the product is not any less expensive than what the victim could find on his or her own; at the worst the information being requested to complete the transaction may contain the name of the business and other information that can be misappropriated.

Bold thieves in the United Kingdom routinely steal business identities by filing fraudulent documents with the country's public registry. These documents are based on information from legitimate businesses. Once registered, the information can be used to steal the name, address and other details about the business to order merchandise, divert mail deliveries and even arrange new business deals.

Business thieves normally target businesses in one of two ways:

Different Forms of Theft 111

- They will steal important information from the business—especially the business identification number—to intercept mail from the business, order merchandise on the business account and send out fake invoices.
- Business thieves will hack into the business computer system to steal information about customers and employees, including their credit card and National Insurance numbers.

Not all business identity theft is done in a high-tech fashion. Often thieves can steal business information the old fashioned way: by going through the business's trash bins, intercepting outgoing mail or wandering through the office and picking up items from desks.

Most business identity theft is committed by businesses' employees. Although many businesses have procedures and guidelines to stop other types of theft–everything from the theft of boxes of paper clips to the embezzlement of funds–they often overlook the possibility of their employees stealing either the business's identity or the identities of fellow employees.

There are several ways that a business might discover that its business identity has been stolen.

- A customer calls to complain about a rude employee or not receiving a product that he or she ordered.
- The business owner receives bills for goods and services that were never ordered.

- People call about a non-existent job opening.
- An unknown person calls about the status of a paycheque they have not received.
- The company receptionist receives calls for an employee who does not work at the business.

The effects of identity theft on a business can be just as devastating as it can be for an individual.

- According to the FSA businesses suffer losses from identity theft of almost $50 billion per year.
- The theft of business identity can result in a significant loss of productivity while employees strives to repair the damage from the theft.
- Businesses may lose long-standing customers whose identities have been stolen as a result of their relationship with the business or because they have been hounded by fraudsters requesting payment for goods or services they never ordered.
- A business's reputation can suffer greatly if customers or employees believe that the business was negligent in protecting their identities.

In addition, although it does not involve the theft of a business identity, many businesses are feeling the fallout from phishing. If phishers are using the company name and logo in a legitimate-looking–but fraudulent–e-mail, the company will have to spend time answering complaints about the phishing attempt.

The Solutions

Instruct your employees to never respond to any unsolicited e-mails regarding your bank accounts and do not click on any links in such e-mails. Never use e-mail or fax to transmit your business's Identification information or any passwords or PINs you use in the course of your business.

Shred all sensitive documents and records before you dispose of them. Scrub the hard drives of any computers you plan to sell or dispose of. You can hire companies to clean out your files and computers on a regular basis and properly dispose of the material that is no longer needed.

Do not acquire or keep unnecessary information. Many businesses are tempted to acquire a lot of information about their customers and keep it on file longer than is really needed. This makes it easier for a fraudster, especially an employee, to gain access to the information and use it for a lengthy period of time before the theft is discovered. If you do not need the information after the initial use, properly dispose of it.

Keep security at the top of your mind when getting rid of any records. Paper records should be stored under lock and key and available to only a few trusted employees. Shred documents you no longer need. Use an alarm system for your business when no one is there. Computer records should be guarded by passwords that are not widely known. Do not let customers or visitors to your business wander through your business's private areas.

Make your employees aware that your customers' identity can be stolen in the course of a normal transaction. They should ask that a customer's National Insurance number only be written down on a form; the customer should never be asked to provide the number aloud. If they call up a customer's information on a computer screen, the screen should be not viewable by other customers.

Make sure you collect keys from former employees when they leave the company and eliminate their passwords from the computer system. If you have to terminate an employee, consider changing the locks or alarm codes to your business as well.

Make sure your IT system is protected by the latest anti-virus and anti-spyware software. If you have an IT system administrator, inform him or her that you want to be alerted immediately if he or she perceives the company is being phished or if unauthorised users are trying to enter your local area network or LAN.

Treat any unsolicited requests for information about your business, employees or customers with great suspicion. Call the company or government agency requesting the information and verify that it is a valid request. If no contact phone number is provided, ignore the request.

Check the monthly statements you receive from your suppliers and your financial institutions carefully to see if any unauthorised activity has occurred.

Finally, make sure you remove the hard drive from any computers you may donate, trash or retire. Information is readily retrievable from computer drives even if the company scrubs or erases a hard drive. Business fraudsters will target companies that sell used or no longer needed equipment with the idea in mind to gain proprietary business information.

Theft of Your Children's Information

Your children are just as vulnerable to identity theft as you are. Thieves can obtain your children's National Insurance numbers, cell phone numbers and even credit card numbers. Fraudsters using phishing or pretexting are just as likely to try to obtain information from your children as they are from you. Once they have obtained this information, they will misuse it just as they would any identity information. Even though your children may not have credit cards or financial accounts that can be mishandled, their identity can be used in other creative ways by thieves. Parents must make their children aware of the real possibility of identity theft and let them know what they can do to minimize the risk and to promptly detect the problem if their identities are stolen.

Recent studies have shown that people under the age of 29 have become the number one demographic for identity theft, accounting for the majority of identity thefts in the last few years. Most people under that age do not discover their identity has been stolen until they try to get a driver's licence or apply for credit. Fraudsters may have had many years to misappropriate a child's identity before the theft is discovered.

Often a minor's identification will be stolen to apply for a driver's licence, especially if the applicant is an illegal immigrant who has purchased the information or a relative of the minor who has had his or her driver's licence revoked. Identity theft of a minor is also a way for terrorists to establish a fake identity.

Fraudsters can take advantage of the tragic death of a child by going back into newspaper or death records to find a deceased child who would have been close to the thief's age. The thief will then counterfeit identification documents or purchase a legitimate birth certificate through legal channels.

It is interesting to note that credit reporting bureaus do not share information. If the age on the first credit application is listed as 23, whether legitimate or fraudulent, that age will stay on the credit report until specifically disputed.

Signs of identity theft of children are very much the same as for adults, such as unusual credit activity or loss of funds from a financial account. However, there are additional ways to recognise that a child's identity has been stolen.

- A parent discovers a child's National Insurance number has been stolen when they try to open a savings account or college fund for the child. They will find there already is an account open under that National Insurance number or the account they wish to open will be denied due to a record of bad cheques.
- The child receives an unusual number of pre-approved credit card offers.
- A teenager is denied a driver's licence because someone else has a licence with that National Insurance number.

The theft of a child's identity may not be by a stranger but rather by a relative or close family friend with access to personal information about the child. Sometimes parents will steal their child's identity if they have destroyed their own credit or lost their driver's licence.

Just because your child receives a pre-approved credit card offer does not mean he or she has had their identity compromised. This offer may result from a teenager applying for a college loan or if you have opened a college fund for him.

You cannot assume a credit card company, phone company or financial institution will not accept an application from someone they think is not of legal age. A fraudster using a child's information will not be revealing the age of the applicant and as far as the company knows, the person applying for credit, a phone or to open a bank account is a legally responsible adult.

Scholarship scams are becoming an increasingly popular way of stealing a teenager's identification. The college-bound teenager without much money is particularly vulnerable to offers of a guaranteed scholarship that requires a processing fee and some of the applicant's personal information. The scholarship is a fraud: The application fee will be pocketed by the fraudster, and the personal information may be used for identity theft.

Children, including teenagers, do not always have the same skepticism as an adult. They are more likely to respond to phishing e-mails, to open unsolicited e-mail attachments or to respond to fraudulent phone calls.

The burden of investigating and cleaning up the effects of the identity theft of a child will fall to the parents. They will, additionally, have to prove they are in a position of legal authority over the child and have the right to correct the situation.

The emotional effects of identity theft can be much stronger in children or teenagers than in adults. This may trigger their first realization that the world is not safe, and as a result they may feel that they have no control of their lives. If the theft was carried out by a family member, a feeling of betrayal can be added on to the other emotional toll.

The Solutions

Do not automatically submit your child's birth certificate or National Insurance number to anyone running an after-school or sports programme. If the coach or counselor needs to see them, show them and put them back into a secure receptacle. If the papers have to be retained, make sure there are copies made and you receive the original. Also, ask about the security measures involved in storing the information.

Just as with your own NI card, do not carry your children's cards with you and make sure they are stored in a secured location in your home.

College students should request, whenever possible, that they be issued a college ID number that is not their National Insurance number so they will not have to constantly submit their National Insurance number for school purposes.

Communicate with your older children about the importance of not giving out personal information to anybody unless they are sure the information will not be misused. Emphasise they should never give this information in response to any unsolicited e-mails or phone calls. Make sure your older children are aware of the importance of securing any paper documents that contain personal information.

Tell your teenagers to never respond to any unsolicited offers for a scholarship. Tell them to alert you to any offer so that you can make sure the offer is legitimate. In most cases, it will not be.

Make sure you have a copy of your child's birth certificate. It is quite likely you will need it to send to credit bureaus, credit card companies and financial institutions to prove your child's identity has been misused by an adult. Be prepared to point out that your child is a minor by law and cannot enter into any contract.

There is no reason why you cannot request a credit report for your child. Although, it is likely the credit bureau will tell you there is no report available, if there is a report available on your child showing credit activity that you and your child

Different Forms of Theft 121

did not initiate, you can safely assume your child's identity has been stolen.

If your child's identity has been stolen, tell other family know members what has happened. If the fraudster is a member of the family, it is possible that he or she will try to appropriate the identity of other family members. Your family members need to know there is a possibility that their identities will be stolen.

If you think a family member has been involved in the identity theft, do not let law enforcement officials pressure you to resolve the issue in a family court. If you choose to prosecute, you have every right to pursue it as a criminal matter.

Keep the emotional health of your child in mind as you combat the effects of the identification theft.

- Identity theft from a stranger can make your child feel unsafe in the world. Let him or her know that criminals exist but that they cannot control the way we live.

- Unless your child is old enough to understand what is occurring, do not involve your child in the details of combating the identity theft. Pitch the discussion regarding the theft to your child's age and maturity.

- Let your child know that this crime occurred despite the fact that they did nothing wrong. Tell them that adults are just as likely to be victims of identity theft, and thieves are very clever in deceiving potential victims.

- Keep your emotions under check when discussing the crime with your child. Expressions of anger or frustration from you can easily transfer to the child and lead to him or her acting out over the incident.
- Tell your children that no physical harm is going to come to them. Fraudsters are not going to kidnap them or rob the house; they are only using the identity for illegal financial gain.

Although changing a NI number for an adult is a very tricky business, doing so for a child may be a very possible solution. The child has not established any credit and will not lose any college or financial records. Most children under the age of 18 have very little to lose by changing their NI numbers.

Mortgage Fraud & Identity Theft

Fraudsters have moved beyond using your identity for mere fraud, such as credit card purchases or opening a new account in your name. Today, fraudsters are using your information to steal the most valuable thing you own: your home and its mortgage. You must be aware of what is involved in using your stolen identity to hijack your mortgage, how prevalent the crime has become, who is typically perpetrating the crime and what you can do to guard yourself against the loss of your home.

Different Forms of Theft

Mortgage fraud is a phenomenon that has been escalating rapidly over the last 5 years and is becoming more and more sophisticated in its methods.

Sadly, most mortgage frauds are aimed at senior citizens or homeowners with mental disabilities. The fraudster knows that these people may be more likely to believe what they are told and act on it. It is a despicable practise, but preying on the elderly and weak has long been popular with con artists of all kinds.

Other common victims of mortgage fraud are people who-due to an unexpected financial problem or an increase in the amount of their monthly mortgage payment due to an adjustable rate mortgage-are having problems making their mortgage payments and facing possible foreclosure.

People who engage in mortgage fraud are not your typical fraudsters. The nature of the fraud necessitates a certain daring and the ability to pose convincingly as a legitimate businessperson. Mortgage fraud criminals run the gamut from actual businessmen to street gangs who are becoming more and more sophisticated in how they commit crime.

There are several different ways a criminal can carry out mortgage theft. Some involve identity theft as a primary element of the crime, but others do not. You should be aware of the most common methods used to commit mortgage fraud.

- A fraudster may be able to reroute your mail pertaining to your home mortgage to the fraudster's address. The fraudster can then use this information to attempt to prove he or she is the real owner of the house and even attempt to have you evicted.

- Your identity information can be used by a fraudster to take out a second loan on your home without your knowledge. By the time you realise what has happened, you could be liable for the payments on this second mortgage or home equity loan.

- Bold fraudsters will drive through neighbourhoods looking for homes owned by elderly people. They know these homes will probably have the most equity built up. The fraudster checks public records regarding the home. Some thieves may actually come to the door posing as a real estate agent and manage to pry sensitive information about the home from the victim. The fraudster then uses the information to fraudulently apply for a home equity loan.

- In some extreme cases, victims of mortgage theft may even have their homes sold out from under them. This usually involves one fraudster posing as a home buyer and the other as a home seller. The buyer approaches a lending institution to apply for a loan to buy the home of the bogus seller. Once the loan is approved, they split the money and disappear.

- Nominee/straw buyer scams involve concealing the identity of the borrower by using stolen identity information. The stolen identity is used to hide the actual applicant's name and credit history from the lender.

- Equity skimming uses false credit reports and income statements based on stolen identity to secure a loan to purchase property. The buyer then signs the property over to the fraudster through a deed that provides no guarantee to title. The so-called investor never pays the mortgage and makes money for months by renting the property until it is foreclosed upon.

- Silent second allows the buyer to borrow a down payment from a seller through a non-disclosed second mortgage. This con makes the primary lender believe the borrower is using his or her own money for the investment.

- Property flipping, one of the most popular forms of mortgage fraud, involves the property being purchased at a higher value then the current equity and quickly resold. This is more complicated because it will usually requires more people being involved in the scam, such as appraisers, buyers, real estate brokers and employees of title companies. These people usually receive some type of kickback from the sale.

- Foreclosure schemes are aimed at homeowners whose houses are already in foreclosure. They are solicited to transfer the deed to the fraudster and do so in the belief they are saving their homes. All the fraudster will do is re-mortgage the property and pocket any exorbitant fees paid by the homeowner.

It may be easier for a fraudster to take out a home equity loan in your name rather than some of the other cons. The documentation is not as extensive for a home equity loan compared with applying for a second mortgage and, often, a home equity loan does not require your home to be reappraised. For example, some lenders do not require a reappraisal if the home equity loan is less than one percent of the value of your home.

If fraudsters have accurate information about your identity and your home mortgage, they can still commit mortgage fraud by filling out false information on lending applications and simply forging your signature.

Technology has made it easier for those committing mortgage fraud. Many lending transactions are handled by phone, fax, e-mail or conventional mail with no face-to-face meeting between the lender and the borrower. This anonymity makes it much easier for a fraudster to hide using these methods.

The Solutions

While it can be distressing to find out that a lender has been fleeced and your home was sold without your knowledge, the lender is the one out the money. You should not be expected to pay the money back, and you will not lose your home.

Different Forms of Theft

Do not even consider any offer you receive that sounds anything like we will buy your house, we can save your credit or we will get you a new mortgage with lower monthly payments. With come-ons like these, you are probably being solicited for some type of scam.

You should never sign away your home without advice of a reliable lawyer. By signing any documents, you may be removing your own name from the deed for your house and allowing someone else to put their name on it instead. This scam can lead to your losing your home.

If you have trouble making your mortgage payments, call your mortgage company or lender and tell them that you are having trouble making your payments. Do not fall for offers that sound too good to be true. Lenders will usually work with you because they lose money in foreclosure actions. They are not simply interested in taking your home. When you call, ask for the mitigation department.

The following actions should be a red flag. Have the good sense to say no to anyone who:

- Calls him- or herself a mortgage consultant, foreclosure service consultant or something similar;
- collects fees before giving you any services;
- advertises to homeowners who are listed for foreclosure;

- advertises services by delivering flyers door to door or posts notices on utility poles; and
- requires you to make your mortgage payments directly to him or her instead of to the lender.

Do not be pressured into signing any type of contract. Take your time to review the document and have it reviewed by your lawyer. And, do not sign any paper that has blank spaces. These could be filled in later by the fraudster to complete the crime.

Get everything in writing, no matter how trivial. If someone making you an offer regarding your home or mortgage just wants to rely on a verbal agreement, shy away from this offer. A reputable businessperson will be happy to provide written documentation as a way to protect both of you in the future.

If you do suspect you were approached by an identity or mortgage fraudster regarding your home or mortgage, contact your mortgage lender and notify your local police station. They are very interested in this type of white-collar crime and will investigate.

Bankruptcy Fraud & Identity Theft

Bankruptcy is generally viewed as a stigma to be avoided at all costs. And, indeed, declaring bankruptcy can have a negative affect on your credit for 1 to 15 years. However, bankruptcy should be viewed as a means to get out of overwhelming debit, an attempt to be as fair as possible with your creditors and a chance to start over.

Bankruptcy can also be misused by fraudsters who can use your identity information to declare bankruptcy and eliminate most of their debt. Other fraudulent bankruptcies that are filed victimize businesses. Whether you are a consumer who discovers your identity has been used to declare bankruptcy or you run a business that could be damaged by bankruptcy fraud, you need to know the basic facts about bankruptcy, how you can be damaged when the process is misused and what you can do to protect yourself.

As in the case of many identity thefts, the perpetrator of bankruptcy fraud is often a family member, particularly one who has access to identity information about a minor. This theft may be designed to put a stay on a certain asset–meaning the asset, usually a house, cannot be liquidated by the bankruptcy court to pay outstanding debts.

In many cases, a bankruptcy fraud is perpetrated as an attempt by a fraudster to forestall detection of a long series of fraudulent unpaid bills.

There are several other methods of using identity theft for the purposes of bankruptcy fraud.

- Transferring property into the name of a relative or friend, and then filing for bankruptcy using the victim's name and National Insurance number to avoid foreclosure; and
- filing for bankruptcy using a false name or National Insurance number that was seemingly chosen at random, because it does not belong to a person known to the perpetrator.

Bankruptcy fraud is only one aspect of a complicated scheme of misusing your identity. This scheme includes opening false accounts, making unauthorised activity on your account and emptying your financial accounts. Often, a false declaration of bankruptcy is the final step in the malicious activities of fraudsters.

Bankruptcy does not just affect the victim of the fraud. Often, the use of fake identity will involve the establishment of a bogus business that will defraud suppliers of goods and services and then declare bankruptcy in the name of the identity theft victim.

The impact of this type of fraud is millions of dollars every year, and the businesses affected are usually not able to recoup their losses.

The Solutions

If you legitimately file for bankruptcy, you must research what is involved and what are the potential there is that this action can be used by others to commit fraud against you or a business. Many Websites provide information about bankruptcy, and legitimate credit counseling agencies can give you guidance or you can consult a lawyer specializing in bankruptcy.

Seeing a bankruptcy report on a credit card may be a lure for fraudsters to approach the person who has declared bankruptcy with bogus offers of new credit. While it is possible you can receive new credit-usually at exorbitant interest rates or with a lower credit limit-many of these offers are fraudulent and designed only to fleece you out of application fees or receive identity information from you. Thoroughly check out whether these offers are legitimate, and, as usual, if it sounds too goods to be true, it probably is.

After you declare bankruptcy, expect to be solicited by credit reporting bureaus who will offer to repair your credit, get you new credit cards and deal with any other creditors whose accounts are still open after you declare bankruptcy. In almost all cases, these are bogus offers from companies that cannot do anything that you cannot do yourself. In some cases, the companies will use the information you provide them to steal your identity.

Credit vigilance using your credit reports–either by yourself or by a credit monitoring service–is one of your best protections against a false bankruptcy in your name by a fraudster. Sometimes, victims of bankruptcy fraud through identity theft may not know about it until they receive a letter requiring them to report to a bankruptcy hearing.

Most times, bankruptcy fraud based on identity theft will not be noticed by bankruptcy professionals or officials until the victim notifies law enforcement of the fraud. But, there are some early warning signs they will look for and you should be aware of.

- A debtor's failure to bring a purported joint debtor to meet with bankruptcy counsel. Sometimes the scammer will ask to take the petition home to have a spouse sign it, and forge the signature without the spouse's knowledge.

- A debtor's failure to appear at the required debtors notification meeting, an initial step in the bankruptcy process.

- The same real property listed in different bankruptcy cases, indicating the perpetrator is filing several cases of bankruptcy in multiple false names to avoid foreclosure on the property.

- Bankruptcy petitions filed serially in the same or neighbouring jurisdictions that carry either (1) the same names but different NI numbers, (2) the same names with different middle initials or (3) slightly different forms of the same name.

If you have filed bankruptcy and believe you have been the victim of identity theft, you should immediately report the case to the nearest Official Receiver's Office.

- Moving to dismiss a pending case in which the bankruptcy filer used a false name or NI number.

- Moving to expunge or void a pending or closed case, thus eliminating it from your credit record.

- Moving to correct the debtor's NI number in the bankruptcy court record.

- Placing the burden upon the bankruptcy filer to amend the petition or correct the NI number, obtaining a court order that the true holder of the number did not file the case and to serve that order on the three major credit reporting bureaus.

- Assisting law enforcement agencies investigating the identity theft.

International Identity Theft

Travelling exposes you to all numerous types of risk of identity theft, partly as a result of the aspects of travel that make it a unique experience and partly because there is an increased likelihood that you may be distracted, confused, or sleep deprived when travelling.

Certainly, you can have your identity misappropriated if you are travelling within the United Kingdom, and the efforts you will make to correct the problems resulting from any instance of identity theft can be frustrating. However, this frustration takes on new dimensions if the identity theft occurs while you are travelling abroad, whether for business or pleasure. There are certain universal rules for protecting your identity no matter where you are, but there are other things you must consider if you are outside the country. Understanding the basics is the first step, but you must also know what unique challenges you might face if your identity is stolen while you are travelling abroad and how to deal with them.

One of the most important documents you will carry with you when you travel abroad is your passport. Passports are issued for a period of 10

Different Forms of Theft

years (for adults; 5 years for children) by the Home Office Identity & Passport Service and will include important identity information about you as well as an identifying photograph. Sometimes you will make frequent use of your passport while you are in a foreign country, while other times you will only need it when you are going through customs as you enter it.

Since September 11, 2001, some embassies can no longer issue new passports. Instead, if your passport is lost or stolen, the staff will issue you a temporary passport if you can provide proper proof of your identity. A new replacement passport will need to be reissued after you return home.

A copy of your passport will contain much of the information that a consular agent will need, including your name, birthday, place of birth, passport number and the date and place where your passport was issued. However, there are still other pieces of information you should be prepared to provide, including:

- An affidavit or a police report regarding the loss or theft describing the circumstances under which your passport was lost or stolen.
- A Citizen Verification and Name Clearance, usually acquired by consular staff though its Passport Verification System.

- Some type of proof of identity, such as a driver's licence. However, even if all your identity papers are stolen, the embassy or consulate has other relatively simple ways to verify your identity.

Embassies and consulates are typically closed on weekends and holidays, so do not expect to be able to obtain a temporary passport at those times. However, the embassy should have an off-hours duty officer who can give you information, or–if you are scheduled to return to the UK imminently–may be able to issue a transportation letter alerting your airline and customs agent that you are attempting to enter the country without a passport.

Credit card companies have security systems that scan transactions for unusual activity. This activity may include several large purchases or purchases that have taken place outside the United States. Based on their security protocols they may try to contact you to determine the transactions are genuine. If you cannot be reached, the company may put a stop on your account and require you to call their security office the next time you try to use the card.

Although you will likely want to use your credit cards for large purchases, you will probably need to carry cash with you. In general, it is much safer to carry traveler's cheques than cash. Traveler's cheques can be used almost anywhere, will not need to be in the country's currency and can be canceled and replaced if they are lost or stolen.

Pickpockets look for tourists, usually identifying them by their garish clothing or abundance of jewelry. These pickpockets work in teams and–while an accomplice jostles you, asks for directions or the time, points to something spilled on your clothing or creates a disturbance–the actual pickpocket has stolen your property. A child or even a woman carrying a baby can be a pickpocket. You must be aware of who is around you at all times!

Instead of coming home to a pile of mail, have it held by your local post office. Or, if you are planning to be in a single location for an extended period of time, you can even have your mail delivered to you overseas. General Delivery services at post offices in most countries will hold your mail. Although embassies and consulates will not handle your mail, some banks and international credit card companies will handle mail for their customers. Decide which option would be best for you.

The Solutions

Opinions vary about the best way to secure your passport when you are in a foreign country. Some believe it is better to keep your passport on your person at all times, especially if you think you may need it. However, this could allow a pickpocket to gain access to your passport. Other experts think you should keep a passport hidden in your hotel room.

Of course, this means an intruder or member of the hotel staff may be able to steal your passport while you are out of the room. In general, if your room has a safe with a changeable combination or the hotel has a safe for guests' valuables, it is probably preferable to leave your passport in a safe at your hotel rather than carry it on your person unnecessarily.

Before your trip, make several copies of the passport identity information (the first two pages of the passport) and keep them separate from your actual passport. Leave one at home before you leave the country, and perhaps carry one in a money belt. These copies will not substitute for a real passport, but having them will make it easier for the U.S. embassy or consular staff to issue you a new passport should yours be lost of stolen.

If your passport is lost or stolen while you are travelling abroad, you should apply for a new passport immediately. Expect to be charged a routine passport fee for a replacement passport. If your money was also stolen, you will be asked to supply the names of someone you believe would be able to assist you financially.

It is usually a good idea to alert your credit card companies in advance of your travel plans. You can do this over the phone to their security office, via e-mail or by written letter. Document your notification in case the credit card company decides your foreign transactions are suspicious even despite your notification.

The rules that apply for using credit cards while travelling abroad are very similar to the ones you would use on a daily basis. They include:

- Only carry one or two credit cards. Leave the rest secured in a hotel safe.

- Use a credit card instead of a debit card. Your liability with a credit card company in case of fraudulent activity will usually be limited to $50 to $100.

- Report any loss or theft of a credit card immediately to the credit card company. Make sure they immediately block any activity on the card.

When you carry your passport and credit cards on your person, place them in different inside pockets. Do not carry these items in handbags, fanny packs or backpacks. If you must carry them in a bag of some sort, your best options are either a shoulder bag with the strap across your chest or, better yet, a secure money belt that is worn under your clothing.

Although it may seem daunting to do so in a foreign country, you should consider filing a police report on any lost or stolen identity information. Most police in larger cities will have an English-speaking officer to assist you. This report can be very important to you in securing a temporary passport as well as when you return home and begin fixing the effects of identity theft.

To avoid scrambling to locate the embassy or consulate, request Consular Information Sheets before you leave by calling the Foreign & Commonwealth Office at 020 7008 1500, or by going online to *www.fco.gov.uk*.

When you first enter a foreign country, you may be asked to fill out a police card listing your name, passport number, destination, local address and reason for travel. Also, depending on local laws, you may be required to leave your passport overnight at the hotel front desk so local police officials can check it. If the hotel does not return your passport the following morning, report the impoundment immediately to the local police and your embassy or consulate.

To learn more before you travel, visit:

Travelocity, *www.travelocity.com*

The Well-Informed Traveler, *www.armchair.com.*

Part 3

FUTURE PROTECTION

Protect Yourself While Travelling Internationally

International travel presents unique challenges in protecting your identity. The actions involved in travelling and staying in overseas hotels make you and your identity vulnerable to clever thieves. You will be showing your passport to a variety of individuals. You will be using your credit cards to make purchases. You will be transporting valuable items and storing them in places with which you are not familiar. Although international travel can be challenging for protecting your identity, you should not allow fear of identity theft to prevent you from travelling. Savvy travelers use the same identity protection techniques while travelling as they use at home so that they can enjoy the experience of international travel with as little fear as possible.

You may naturally have your guard down when you are on vacation. You obviously want to relax and enjoy your environment, whether you are sightseeing or just lying on the beach or next to the pool. Fraudsters count on travelers being less vigilant while they are on vacation and will prey on this.

In addition, when you are travelling internationally, you need to protect a form of identification that you do not have to worry about normally: your passport. You will need a valid passport both to enter another country and then to return home again. You can expect to have to show it when you pick up your ticket at your departure airport and again when you arrive at your destination. You may occasionally need it to prove your identification if you are making a purchase in another country by credit card.

If you plan on driving in another country you will need to acquire an international driver's licence from either the Automobile Association (AA) or The Royal Automobile Club (RAC). It is important to use the services of a reputable organisation. Otherwise, the business you choose may use the information you provide for your application to steal your identity and not provide you with a valid driver's licence at all.

An international driver's licence can be used for identification purposes in a foreign country, but they are also gateways to gaining access to a tremendous

Future Protection 143

amount of identification information about you, just as your domestic driver's licence is.

Credit card companies do monitor transactions and will pay special attention to any unusual charges or if the credit card has been used many times in one day. This is especially true if the activity originates overseas.

Phone card fraud is a very real concern when travelling in a foreign country. Many travelers will use a phone card to make calls within the country or back home. These cards offer very attractive rates per minute and make it more convenient to use public phones. However, be aware that shoulder surfers will watch you punch in your phone card number, memorize it and use it later to make fraudulent calls or open a new phone account.

Hotel security can vary widely depending on where you are staying. Ideally, there will be a safe in your hotel room to store valuables and important aspects of your identification such as your passport or credit cards. If there is, use it. If not, the hotel itself should have a safe to store these items for you.

Opinions vary as to whether you should carry your passport with you when you are away from your hotel room. Some believe it is a good idea to keep your passport with you at all times, both to secure your passport and also to use as identification if necessary. Others believe you should not carry your passport with you–in case you are a victim of a pickpocket or purse thief–but rather keep it secured in your hotel. The bottom line is that you should do whatever you feel most comfortable with, because crime patterns and your needs for identification will vary from place to place and from trip to trip.

Fraudsters will often pose as an employee of the hotel and call you–usually at a late hour when you are unlikely to be really alert–to request a verification of your credit card number and expiration date. The information will be used to make unauthorised charges on your credit card.

Even with the best security measures, theft from hotel rooms does occur. Often, the thieves are cleaning or maintenance employees of the hotel who have access to your room when you are not there. They will be looking for valuables as well as identification that can be stolen and either used by them or sold to fraudsters.

Thieves who access your hotel room will not just be looking for hard copies of identification, such as a passport, international driver's licence or National Insurance number. They will also access your portable computer and either steal information from it or steal the computer itself.

Airports are prime hunting grounds for pickpockets and purse thieves. Thieves know travelers are distracted and harried while maneuvering through an airport and may not be paying attention to everything going on around them. They also know that some travelers are careless about leaving bags unattended at a gate.

The Solutions

Vigilance is especially important when you travel internationally. You must be aware of what is going on around you at all times and believe that anyone may be looking to steal your identity.

Never leave your bags unattended in an airport. Always carry your identity information and boarding pass with you, and do not keep them in a bag that can be easily stolen.

Your luggage can be stolen at any time while you are travelling, even by employees of the airline you are using. Many travel experts suggest you avoid the real problem of lost or stolen luggage by shipping your bags ahead of time via a service such as UPS or FedEx.

Before making a hotel reservation, ask what security measures the hotel has for stored items. Ask them if they have safes in the hotel rooms or what procedures they have in place to safeguard items in a hotel safe. If you are not comfortable with the answers you receive, consider finding another hotel.

If someone calls your hotel room and asks for your credit card number, never provide it, no matter how the person identifies himself. Call back, but make sure you call a number you have looked up yourself, not any number that the caller provides.

Consider using only one credit card while you are travelling internationally so you can more easily check the bill later for unauthorised charges.

Alert whatever credit card company you plan to use while travelling that you will be overseas and may be using your card more than usual. This will prevent the company from putting a hold on your card because they are detecting unusual activity on it.

Make copies of the credit cards and debit cards–front and back–that you plan to take with you and leave the copies in a secure place at home. If any of your cards are stolen, you will have the information handy to remedy the situation when you return.

Make a copy of your passport and birth certificate and keep it in a separate place. In the event you lose your passport, you will have a copy, including your passport number and birth certificate to take to the nearby consulate or embassy. With that information they can quickly provide you with a replace passport.

Future Protection

Only use your debit card for ATM withdrawals. If your credit card number is stolen, your liability is limited for any of the unauthorised purchases made on it. If your debit card number is stolen, a fraudster can access your bank accounts and empty them. You might consider asking your bank to put a withdrawal limit temporarily on your accounts to avoid large unauthorised withdrawals. Make sure your debit card PIN is only four digits. Some ATMs will not accept PINs longer than four numbers.

Just as you would while at home, do not carry any more identification with you than is necessary. For instance, do not carry your NI card with you.

Be aware of who is around you when you are using a phone card at a public phone or your debit card at an ATM. Shoulder surfers in other countries are just as likely to monitor your key strokes as they would in the United States. There is no reason to be embarrassed about shielding a phone pad or ATM keypad while you are punching in your numbers.

Unless absolutely necessary, do not have any identification information stored on a portable computer that you plan on taking with you during your travels.

Consider contacting these resources for international driver's licence information.

Automobile Association (The AA)

Royal Automobile Club (RAC)
Green Flag Motoring Assistance Recovery Club

The New Services Banks Provide

Financial institutions do not include just banks. Savings and loan associations and credit unions also offer savings accounts, chequeing accounts and loans. Depending on the size of the institution and the scope of services it provides, it may not offer the type of security that you feel is necessary for your accounts.

Many people will open a credit card issued by the same financial institution with whom they have their other financial accounts. People believe this will make it more efficient to keep track of their financial activities.

Larger financial institutions will offer online banking services. These services will allow you to view your account activity on a daily basis. Many times online banking will also allow you to view the activity and balances of any credit cards you hold through the bank.

Your financial institution can provide you with a wide variety of services, but it may also share your identity information with other companies and their affiliates. You must expect that this can happen.

Automated teller machines, or ATMs, have become very familiar. They require the use of an ATM card and your personal PIN to access the ATM. Your ATM card may also be a debit card. This will allow you to pay for purchases at any companies that accept standard credit cards.

Many financial institutions now allow your employer to directly deposit your regular cheques into a specified account. In a similar fashion, you can also authorise direct withdrawals from your account for the payment of monthly bills, such as utility bills, club memberships, and donations to nonprofits.

A new service offered by financial institutions is electronic cheque conversion. This process converts a paper cheque into an electronic payment at the point of purchase or when the company receives the cheque in the mail. When the cheque is processed, you will be asked to sign a receipt authorizing the merchant to present the cheque to your financial institution electronically and authorise the funds be placed in his account.

The Solutions

Before you open an account with any financial institution or establish an Electronic Fund Transfer service (non paper transaction, such as moving money at an ATM), or EFT, whether it is a bank, savings and loan or credit union, you need to inquire about their security practises. Be sure to ask these questions:

- What type of password and user ID do you require?
- What online security measures, including encryption, do you have?
- What is the name, phone number and address of the person I should notify if I believe unauthorised activity has occurred on my account?
- Can you provide documentation of my right to receive documentation of transfers and information about how to stop payment on a pre-authorised transfer?
- Can you provide a statement on how you might share my information with other financial institutions or commercial businesses?
- What is the limit that I would be charged if there was unauthorised activity on my credit card?

While there is nothing wrong with carrying a credit card with your primary financial institution, you may still want to shop around for a credit card with the highest limit, lowest interest rate and best security measures. Remember, it is always possible that the original credit card company will sell your account to another financial institution, so any perceived or actual advantages can evaporate at any time.

Be very careful when you set-up a direct deposit with your financial institution for your paycheques. Make sure the information you give your company's paymaster is not readily shared with anybody else. Monitor your financial accounts closely to make sure the direct deposit is being made and there is no unauthorised use of your financial accounts.

An automated withdrawal from your financial institution account to pay bills can be a convenience, but it can also cause you some cash-flow problems. You need to monitor your accounts to make sure there are sufficient funds to cover the monthly withdrawals. You may also want to keep a copy of the bill paying schedule as a hard copy or on a electronic spread sheet to make sure you know when these withdrawals will take place. This will also be helpful in determining if an unauthorised person is accessing your financial accounts.

In general, you are at less risk from identity theft if you use a credit card than if you use a debit card for a purchase or other financial transactions. Credit companies have a limit on the liability you will have for unauthorised use of the credit card–usually between $50 and $100–while access to your financial accounts through a debit card purchase could result in a major loss to you.

Your Credit Report

There is no more important part of your credit record than your credit report and resulting credit score. Credit reports are compiled by the major credit bureaus and include the amount of debt you have and a record of how promptly you pay your bills. A credit score is a single number that gives creditors a sense of how much of a credit risk you are compared to the rest of the population.

Reviewing your credit report and credit score is an excellent way for you to determine if your credit has been compromised by a fraudster. You need to know how to access your credit reports and how to recognise clues that could indicate that someone has misused your identity.

Each credit report will contain basic information about you, including.

- Identity information such as your full name, last two addresses, NI number, birthday and place of employment.
- Detailed information about your loans and credit accounts, including the name of the issuer, date the

account was opened, original balance or limit, terms of the account and current balance of the account.

- Public record information including bankruptcies, tax liens, judgments and other filings.

- Credit report requests, recorded in the report as non-evaluated.

- A consumer statement–a space on the report for you to challenge or explain any creditor entry in your account (in 100 words or less).

The status of each item on a credit report is indicated by a complicated code system. An example is CO NOW PAY, which means the account was a charge off, but you are now paying it

Your credit report will probably not include other types of activities, such as utility bills, hospital bills, accounts or loans with credit unions, oil company credit cards and chequeing and savings account information.

Your credit report can be accessed by others for a number of reasons. Your credit report will be reviewed when you:

- Apply for a new credit card;

- attempt to get a mortgage;

- apply for a short-term loan such as for an automobile or for appliances and furniture;

- sign a lease for an apartment; and
- apply for a job.

A credit report is different than a credit score. A credit report includes the information about your identity and credit history. A credit rating, based on this information, is a numeric value also called a credit score. This score is generally a number that falls between 300 and 900. The higher the score, the more easily you will be able to acquire new credit at favourable rates of interest or rent an apartment.

A credit score is derived using information from five different categories:

- The type of credit you use;
- your credit history;
- the amount you currently owe;
- the length of your credit history; and
- new credit obtained.

You will not receive a credit score with your free copy of your credit report; you will have to pay a fee to obtain this information. When you receive your numerical credit score or rating, you will also receive a national percentile ranking reflecting the percentage of the population with scores higher or lower than yours. This information can be helpful to you by helping you anticipate how easy it will be apply for new credit.

Credit reports can include misinformation. Some misinformation can be a result of the activities of identity theft while other misinformation may result from simple inputting errors. Employment information on a credit report, especially the length of time you are employed, is often incorrect. If you are self-employed, check that your status is accurately reflected on your credit report. If it is not–especially if it incorrectly lists you as unemployed–you should have the error corrected immediately.

Indications of identity theft on your credit report will include applications for credit that you did not make, activity on your credit accounts that you did not initiate and indications that you have been turned down for credit.

Fraudsters will use your stolen information to attempt to set-up new credit under your name. Multiple requests for your credit report–including ones generated by a fraudster–can be counted as a strike against you when you apply for credit because the potential creditor may believe you are trying to apply for too much credit.

Your credit report can be accessed by you for no charge once a year. You can also request a copy of your credit report if you are turned down for a loan, a new credit card or an apartment based on your credit rating. You can also request the credit bureau examine what you believe is fraudulent activity and remove it from your credit report.

Many people never access their credit reports even though they can easily do so for free. Often people will check their credit reports once a year, but will not do any follow-up on the information. Fraudsters know this and will take advantage of this delay and inattention to misappropriate your identity.

The Solutions

To give yourself as much protection as possible from identity theft, you should order a copy of your credit report at least twice a year and maybe on a quarterly basis. You can set-up a service with any of the major credit bureaus by which you can check this information online. You will be charged for more than one report a year, unless it is requested because you have been rejected for credit, an apartment or a job based on your credit report.

When you request a copy of your credit report, you will be asked to supply your full legal name, spouse's name, your current and previous addresses, your National Insurance number and birthday. You can request a copy of your credit report in writing or by visiting a credit bureau's Website.

If you have a dispute with any item on your credit report, or believe the report indicates identity theft, you will have to communicate with the credit bureau in writing. One option is to use the space on the printed credit report called a Consumer Statement. Detail any concerns you have about your credit report there and return then return the document to the credit bureau.

You should consider writing a letter by hand to prevent your correspondence being mistaken for a form letter. Credit bureaus will usually not respond to a request to review information if it looks like a boilerplate letter generated from a credit management agency.

If, after reviewing your credit report, you believe your credit has been compromised, avoid using a credit management service to help correct the problem. You can do everything that is required yourself. If you hire a credit management service, you will be paying somebody to do work that you can easily do yourself–and probably more efficiently.

Do not give up if a credit bureau does not respond to your request for more information or your letter refuting negative information. Credit bureaus, by law, have to respond to your requests, but it may take some time. Be prepared to send follow-up letters or make phone calls to get the action you need. The three main consumer credit reporting bureaus include:

CallCredit, Ltd.
Consumer Services Team
P.O. Box 491
Leeds LS3 1WX
t. 0870 060 1414
www.callcredit.co.uk

Equifax, PLC
P.O. Box 1140
Bradford BD1 54S
t. 0870 010 0583
www.equifax.co.uk

Experian, Ltd.
P.O. Box 9000
Nottingham NG80 7WP
t. 0870 241 6212
www.experian.co.uk

Identity Theft Insurance–Is It Worth the Money?

If you have been a victim of identity theft or are concerned about the possibility that it might happen to you, you may be considering purchasing identity theft insurance. Before you take what could be an expensive step, you need to consider whether identity theft insurance will really be worth the

Future Protection 159

investment, what the insurance will actually cover and which type of policy would be best for you.

Not all forms of insurance are created equal. Depending on the type of policy you take out for identity theft, you may not be protected from every type of damage caused by identity theft.

Many insurance carriers will offer some form of identity theft insurance as part of a homeowner's insurance policy. Others will require the extra coverage be taken out as a stand-alone policy or an endorsement to a homeowner or renter's insurance policy. Identity theft insurance will usually cost between $25 and $50 a year for coverage and will provide between $15,000 and $25,000 worth of coverage.

Having identity theft insurance will not spare you from any of the reporting responsibilities that result from being a victim identity theft. You will still need to:

- Contact your credit card companies and financial institutions as well as the credit bureaus to report the theft;
- file a police report regarding the theft; and
- change your PIN numbers and passwords and possibly acquire a new NI number.

Identity theft insurance will not fix your credit rating or pay back money to your accounts. It is not the same as homeowners' or automobile insurance that pays for the repair of damage done to your residence or vehicle. The actual damages from the loss of your identity–such as unauthorised charges or losses to your financial accounts–will either be taken care of by the institution or be your personal responsibility. The loss of such non-financial aspects of your identity such as your National Insurance number will not be covered by insurance.

Identity theft insurance typically covers out-of-pocket expenses involved in dealing with the consequences of identity theft, such as:

- Phone bills for calls made to creditors or financial institutions.
- Lost wages as a result of time needed to correct the problems.
- Fees for reapplying for loans declined due to wrong credit information caused by fraudsters.
- Notary and certified mailing costs for completing and delivering fraud affidavits.
- Some attorney fees.

Paying $25 to $50 a year for identity theft insurance is probably less expensive than what you would pay for credit monitoring, which can typically range from $50 to $100 a year. However, the reimbursement for lost wages under most identity theft insurance may not be adequate for the wages lost by higher-income earners. Reports estimate that most identity theft victims will spend 22 days or more of their work time on remedying the problem. Identity theft insurance typically only reimburses up to $2,000 in lost wages.

You may not need insurance to help cover costs incurred from reversing judgments and criminal records caused by the identity theft.

The Solutions

The best type of identity theft insurance is the system of precautions you implement yourself. Do not be careless in protecting your identity. Only the dangerously cavalier will simply rely on insurance to solve their problems.

Check with your financial institution or credit card company regarding identity theft insurance. Do not assume this coverage is automatic. Sometimes the institution will offer you some type of identification insurance for free, and then charge you an added monthly fee-usually between $3.75 and 6.99 (or $45 to $84 a year)-for extra services, such as:

- Access to credit education specialists.
- Notification of loans or accounts being opened in your name.
- Copies of your credit reports.

- Monitoring of your credit reports 5 days a week with notification of any changes in the credit report

Many major insurance carriers offer some form of identity theft insurance. These include:

- HBOS Group
- SainsburysBank
- CPP (Card Protection Plan)
- Lifelock (www.getlifelock.net)
- BT Identity Protection
- Barclay's
- LloydsTSB
- Natwest

As you would when you shop for any insurance, there are certain questions you should ask an insurance carrier regarding its identity theft coverage.

- What is the annual cost of the policy?
- What specifically does the policy cover?
- Is there a deductible cost I will have to pay?
- What are the coverage limits for the different aspects of the policy?
- Does the policy provide some form of credit monitoring?
- Does the insurance company talk directly with the credit companies to alert them to the ID Theft?

- What will I have to do to file a claim, and what response should I expect?

It may be less expensive to include some type of identity theft insurance with your overall homeowners' or renters' insurance. You may end up paying more for a stand-alone policy.

Although having identity theft insurance can help reimburse you for some of the costs associated with identity theft, it also means you will have add your insurance company to the list of those you need to contact if you suspect identity theft. You will probably have to fill out insurance claim forms just as you would for any other type of loss covered by your insurance.

Do some simple math before you acquire identity theft insurance. You can expect to take approximately 22 work days to remedy identity theft problems. If the reimbursement from your identity theft insurance is well below what your time is really worth, the insurance may not be worth the cost of the premiums.

Of all the aspects of identity theft insurance, the credit monitoring service is perhaps the least important. You can do this yourself. If your insurance does include credit monitoring, make sure the monitoring is occurring on a daily basis and is being done from all three credit bureaus.

Do not expect identity theft insurance to be a cure-all for your problems, especially the emotional affect of identity theft. The insurance, depending on the policy, will help reimburse you for some expenses, but it will not restore the time you lose while dealing with the theft or ameliorate the emotional impact it will have on you and your family.

Setting-Up Fraud Alerts

If you suspect your identity has been compromised and it is being used for fraudulent transactions or to establish new, fraudulent credit accounts, you need to consider setting-up a fraud alert with the three major credit reporting bureaus.

A fraud alert will not protect you from every form of identity theft, but it is a primary tool that you can use to stop the bleeding (so to speak) caused by identity theft. You will need to know what a fraud alert is, how you can file one and what it will do to help remedy your identity theft.

A fraud alert is an action that you take in coordination with the three major credit reporting bureaus. Each of these credit bureaus will have a fraud unit that you can use to place a fraud alert on your report. If you place a fraud alert with one consumer credit reporting agency, the alert will be placed with the other credit bureaus and you will be sent information about receiving copies of your credit reports from the other companies.

When you place a fraud alert on your account, you will have to supply your personal information, including, your name, address and National Insurance number. You will be assigned a unique number for the alert. At this point, you can also request that the credit report carry only the last four digits of your NI number.

Once you request that the credit bureaus put a fraud alert on your records, you should be sent a free credit report that will show that the alert is on your record. At this time, too, the consumer reporting companies will remove your name from the marketing lists for pre-screened credit for 5 years, although you can ask them to put your name back on the lists before the 5 years are over.

Typically, the credit bureaus will keep a fraud alert in effect for 90 to 180 days from the time that you request it be placed on your account. If you choose to, you can have the alert extended to 7 years.

Credit issuers are not required by law to observe fraud alerts. Therefore, a fraud alert is not a cure-all for identity theft. Fraudulent accounts may still be set-up under your name even after you have placed a fraud alert on your credit reports. However, when a business sees that a fraud alert has been placed on your report, an employee may attempt to verify your identity before issuing you credit. As part of this verification process, the business may contact you directly.

By the time you issue a fraud alert on your accounts there may have been a large amount of damage done to your credit or misinformation included in your report as a result of your identity theft. You will still need to address specific issues on your credit report and make the effort needed to refute the misinformation and have it changed.

The Solutions

Check your credit reports about a month after you request the fraud alerts, and review them carefully for signs of activity that you did not initiate, such as:

- New credit accounts that have been opened without your knowledge.
- Purchases made with your credit cards that you did not make.
- Inquiries into your credit that may result from someone using your identity to open a new phone account or rent an apartment.

It may take that long-or longer-for suspicious activity to appear on your credit reports. Maintain vigilance on your credit reports even after you have filed a fraud alert. This alert is not a guarantee that fraudulent activity will not occur on your accounts.

An initial fraud report will only stay on your files for 90 days. If you choose to place an extended alert on your files, which continues the alert for 7 years, you will probably have to file an identity theft report with the credit reporting bureaus. The identity theft report will include a copy of the report you have filed with a federal, state or local law enforcement agency. It may also include specific information required by the credit reporting bureau.

Do not hesitate to request an initial fraud alert if you suspect identity theft. The alert can be removed later if you realise you were mistaken. But, the longer you wait to request the alert, the more likely a thief can victimize you. To make the process of requesting the fraud alert easier, have your information organised and in writing. Make sure you include the personal information you will need to request the alert and notes on why you think your identity has been stolen.

The decision to extend your fraud alert from 90 days to 7 years will be based on the certainty that your identity has been stolen. As mentioned earlier, you will need to include an identity theft report with any request for an extended fraud alert. Before you go to this effort, you may want to take the time to review your credit report at the 1 month point–to confirm you see evidence of fraudulent activity–before asking for the extended alert. When you place an extended alert on your credit reports, you are entitled to two free file disclosures during each 12-month period.

You do not have to wait for proof to request an initial fraud alert be placed on your accounts. You can request this initial alert if you only suspect your identification has been stolen. You may request this based on your wallet or purse being stolen, your house being burglarized or realizing you have been the victim of phishing.

Businesses should try to contact you before issuing you new credit after a fraud alert has been placed on your credit report. To speed that process along, you may want to consider placing a cell phone number in the fraud report. Also, for this reason it is important to keep your personal information current with the credit reporting bureaus. If you change your name, address or phone numbers, you should immediately inform the credit reporting agencies of the change.

Once you are convinced that identity theft and fraud are no longer a matter for immediate concern, you can remove a fraud alert from your credit report. To do so you will have to supply the same personal information you did when you first requested the alert.

Even though you can ask for your name to be put back on pre-screened credit lists after you have filed your fraud report, you should consider keeping your name off these lists. Pre-screened credit solicitations can be stolen from your mail or from your trash. If you wish to open new credit it should be because you initiate the action. Although in many cases of identity theft reporting you will be communicating in writing, you should request your initial fraud alert by calling the credit reporting bureau's fraud line.

Keep careful records when you request the initial or extended fraud alert. Note what date and time you made the initial contact, who you spoke to at the credit reporting bureau, what action they have promised and what follow-up you may need to do.

Fraud Watch International, *www.fraudwatchinternational.com*

Also, if you suspect your identity has been stolen, contact The CIFAS Protective Registration Service provides credit protection services to set up fraud alert protection on your account. The cost to you is a minimal amount of $11.75 annually.

Maximizing Computer Protections

Protecting your identity while you are using your computer and taking the proper precautions to make sure you can recover from an unwanted incursion into your computer are two of the most important elements in preventing identity theft.

Installing effective anti-virus software or firewalls are a good first line of defence against unauthorised access to your computer, but there are other aspects of computer usage as it relates to identity theft that you need to be aware of. You can take steps to protect your computer proactively by being vigilant and using appropriate software. You can also set-up systems that will allow you to survive an attack on your computer and the effort to steal your identity.

You probably know not to open e-mail that appears to be from nobody you know or contains either no subject or a subject that is a string of nonsense words. You realise that opening an attachment within the e-mail may download a virus or spyware onto your hard drive or that even opening the e-mail may start an attack on your computer. What you may not know is that there are many other ways criminals can come at you through your computer either to just cause mischief or to steal your identity information.

- Remote login occurs when an unauthorised person connects to your computer and controls it in some way, ranging from viewing or gaining access to your files to actually running programmes on your computer.

- Application backdoors are programmes that have special features to allow someone to remotely access your computer; others contain bugs that provide a backdoor–or hidden access–that allows for some control of the programme.

- SMTP session hijacking allows spammers to send thousands of messages through another computer, making it difficult to track down the spammer.

- Operating system bugs either fail to provide enough security against remote use of the computer or use the occasional backdoor in the operating system to access the computer, making it easier for a hacker to gain access to your computer.

- Denial of service is a nearly impossible-to-fight technique in which a hacker floods a Website server with unauthorised requests, making the server slow down or even crash because it cannot find the computer that sent the requests.

- Macros were designed to be a benefit to users by allowing them to set-up a complicated series of directions under one command. Hackers create their own macros that can destroy data on your computer or crash your hard drive.

- Spam is usually harmless–similar to junk mail–and is simple to delete from your e-mail inbox. However, it can be dangerous if it contains links to Websites that will send a cookie to your computer allowing a backdoor access.

- E-mail bombs are usually part of a personal attack on your computer in which someone sends you the same e-mail thousands of times until your e-mail system can no longer accept new e-mail.
- Redirect bombs use Internet tools to redirect information through a different router, one of the ways that a denial of service attack is carried out.
- Source routing is an attack in which the source providing a packet of information can arbitrarily determine the path of routers the information goes through. Hackers use this to make it look like their sinister e-mails are being sent by someone you know or trust or even someone who is part of your local area network (LAN) at work.

An emerging and popular trend used by legitimate e-mailer is to use HTML-rendered e-mail. HTML is the basic coding used to set-up text and images on a Webpage. Some e-mailers use this to jazz up their e-mail through the use of different colors, borders and images. These messages looks good, but HTML e-mail contains some real dangers for the people receiving them.

HTML-rendered e-mail:

- Can be full of invisible images, specially formed links and other features that will allow someone to track your e-mail;

- contain active content that will automatically open attachments or download files to your computer system; and

- allows spammers and computer criminals to make dangerous links appear to be from some legitimate source. This is popular in phishing scams.

The Solutions

Many of the attacks listed here cannot be adequately stopped by a firewall. If you accept e-mail, it is inevitable you will receive some spam or potentially dangerous messages. You must combine your common sense and vigilance with the latest technology to provide the best level of protection for your computer.

You can establish different levels of security with a firewall or spam blocker installed as part of your Internet provider service. If you block everything, it defeats the purpose of having an Internet connection, but a good way to establish a workable level of security is to initially set-up your protection to block everything. You can then start modifying the level of security to allow the types of traffic that you want. Another option, especially for the casual computer user, is to initially set-up any security using the defaults of the programme.

Inform your friends and colleagues that you will only open plain text e-mail messages, and explain why this is important to you. Plain text messages:

- Do not support embedded images and effectively squash Web bugs;

- do not support active content and will not allow attachments to open automatically; and

- give you a WYSIWYG–what you see is what you get–experience with no hidden commands. The link displayed is the actual link.

When in doubt regarding opening an e-mail or an attachment or downloading information from a Website, always err on the side of caution and do not download, open or execute any files or e-mail attachments. If you think a download offer from one of your software suppliers is legitimate, check its security site to make sure what has been sent you is not malicious. Wi-fi networks are becoming an increasingly popular way to access the Internet. Among other advantages, these networks allow multiple computers to be online at once, without a hard-wired connection. However, a wi-fi system requires you to use special precautions.

- You can reconfigure your base station to not broadcast constantly the Service Set Identifier, or SSID. A stranger who has learned the name of your wi-fi network can still gain access to it, but this will keep out random users.

- Encrypt your wireless network password, making it much harder for someone to hack into the network.

- Configure the base station to allow only machine access code, or MAC address. Every computer has a unique MAC address, and you can programme your network to accept only your computer's MAC address. While this can be labour intensive, it can pay off later in added security, especially when used in conjunction with the other two suggestions.

Protecting Your Passwords & Choosing Secure Passwords

For every credit and financial transaction and for a variety of online uses, you will need to establish passwords or a personal identification number (PIN)–sometimes along with a separate user ID. This password will allow you to take the actions you want to do–whether it is paying bills, chequeing account activity or transferring funds.

Unfortunately, many people are very careless about how they choose their passwords and how they protect their information. They select an easy-to-remember password and may leave the information in a readily accessible place. Once thieves have fraudulently acquired your passwords, they can use them to do a tremendous amount of mischief. You must know how to create secure passwords and how to keep them safe from criminals.

You can expect to establish and use passwords for many purposes, including:

- Accessing financial information
- Bill paying
- Shopping
- Reviewing credit card balances and transactions
- Reviewing utility bills, such as phone or cable services

For many online transactions you will need to establish both a user ID and a password. Both pieces of information will be required to allow you to make the transaction or access your online information. Often an online service will give you hints on how to set-up a user ID or password based on their knowledge of the possibility of theft. These hints will include suggestions for a user ID or password.

The fact is, we live in a world where we are forced to remember a lot of IDs and passwords, whether for online transactions, ATM transactions or for accessing information over the phone. Because of this, many people tend to use the same user IDs and passwords so they can remember them. Fraudsters know this tendency and will use it to take one user ID and password and use it to gain access to a variety of credit card accounts, phone accounts or financial accounts.

To help remember their various passwords and numbers, many people will carry this information with them. They will write their ATM numbers on their debit cards or their calling card passwords on the actual calling cards. Fraudsters know this and will try to gain access to this information by picking your pocket or stealing your purse.

Passwords are not the same as activation codes. When you receive a new credit card or a renewed card, you will need to call in to the credit card center to activate the card. This will normally require that you to enter the number of the card, the last four digits of your National Insurance number and perhaps some other piece of information such as your mother's maiden name.

Online shopping services are adding to the layers of security to establish an online identity by asking for more information than just your name and National Insurance number.

- Your mother's maiden name;
- the city in which you were born;
- the name of a favorite pet; and
- the name of a child or close relative.

This information may seem secure, but a sophisticated fraudster who has gained access to some form of your identity may be able to find out this information. The fraudster knows these questions will be asked and will be prepared to provide the proper information.

As part of their security statements, most online services should be able to give you some idea of how they protect your user ID and password.

Password protection does not just extend to the user. If fraudsters steal password information they may be able to access secure portions of the online Website and create problems for the business. A secure password can protect an online Website or home page as much as it would for the user.

Sometimes you may be asked for your password or PIN by a friend or relative. When you share this information you are exposing yourself to risk of access by a fraudster.

Falsely accessing a password to a bank account that has little funds in it may seem like no big deal, but for a fraudster, this password could make yourself vulnerable to a much larger identity theft attack that goes beyond simply using this one account.

If you are using an online password that is a common word, you could be vulnerable to a dictionary attack. This is done by sophisticated online thieves who use a dictionary programme to try to guess your password.

Passwords are just as vulnerable to phishing or pretexting. Fraudsters will use these techniques to gain access to a credit card or financial account password just as they would try to get the account number or your National Insurance number. Fraudsters may use shoulder surfing to gain access to your password or PIN when you use an ATM or punch in identification numbers into a public phone.

The Solutions

Although it can make it difficult to remember all your passwords, you should try to use different passwords for different uses. Your PIN for your debit card number should be different than what you would use for an online service. If you need to supply personal information as a verifier for the password, you need to vary this on the different online services you might use.

Consider using mnemonic devices to memorize your password. This will help you avoid using common words that could be accessed by dictionary searching software.

- Intentionally misspelling a word might help protect you from a dictionary attack, but it is no guarantee that sophisticated software will not discover it.

- As an example of a mnemonic method of memorization: instead of using the word hoops as a password, change it to ILTPBB for I like to play basketball or MDRJTN for My Daughter Rose Just Turned Nine.

- Some computer operating systems and online sites will accept these pass phrases instead of a password of letters and numbers.

In most cases with any passwords, your best defence is to use a random combination of numbers and letters instead of any number or word that would be easy to trace to you.

If you use letters as part of a password, consider making them both upper and lower case. Sometimes online passwords are case sensitive, and a fraudster using the wrong combination of upper and lower case letters will not be able to gain access to your account.

Write down your passwords and keep them in a secure location. Do not leave them out in your home, leave them visible on your desk at work or carry them with you in your wallet and purse. Do not tell anyone your passwords and never give them out over e-mail or the phone.

If your ISP offers a choice of authentication systems, see if they offer Kerberos challenge/response or public key encryption rather than simple passwords.

There is computer software available that will help you remember your passwords. Two of the most effective, and safest, are Apple's Keychain and Palm's Secure Desktop.

Be careful if you decide to have an online service remember your password. This information can be vulnerable to hackers. Although it can be more time consuming, you might want to always enter your password when you log on to a sensitive site.

When you create an online password use the entire keyboard and not just the most common letters. Often a password can contain punctuation marks or other symbols on your keyboard rather than just letters and numbers.

If you think your personal information has been compromised, do not hesitate to change all your passwords. Most online services will allow you to change your password at any time. As a general rule, you might consider changing your passwords on a regular basis.

Never enter your passwords on a computer that is not in your control. This would include public computers in Internet cafes or at the library. You should also be very careful about entering passwords on your work computer.

For more information visit:
Microsoft, *www.microsoft.com/athome/security/privacy/password.mspx.*
UF Bridges, *www.erp.ufl.edu/password/tips.html.*

Back-Up Important Files

Not only can your identity be stolen and your credit and financial information be improperly accessed, an identity theft can also result in the malicious destruction of your important files. This could be done by a physical thief who steals your materials and throws them away, or it could involve a hacker using spyware to wipe out your hard-drive records.

There are no guarantees that a thief will not tamper with your files and even destroy them. Your only viable option is to make sure you have a system in place that will allow you to identity what are the files that are most important to you, how you can most efficiently back them up and where you can store them to allow you access if your primary files are compromised.

Most people are very lax about backing-up their files. They may do so when they think of it, which could be once a year or even less often than that. There always seems to be something more important to do than backing-up files!

There are two basic areas you may lose information from important files.

- Your files can be corrupted or lost from the hard drive of your computer.

- Your paper files either at work or at home can be stolen by co-workers or burglars.

Although the mischief caused by fraudsters can result in the loss of information, there are other ways that files can be destroyed, adding to the list of good reasons why it is important to back-up your important files. These include:

- A power surge, which could be caused by a nearby lightning strike during a thunderstorm;
- a power loss while your computer is on;
- although it is rare with newer computers, a mechanical failure in your hard drive can destroy your files; and
- a fire or flood can physically destroy both your computers and your paper files.

Computer files can be attacked from several directions, but the most common culprits are viruses and spyware that you inadvertently download by opening an e-mail or an e-mail attachment.

There is more to backing-up a computer file than simply saving it to a different place on your hard drive. Actually, you need to copy it on a different source–such as a CD–that you store in a different location, away from your computer.

It is up to you to decide which files are important. But, there are some basic files you should consider backing-up. These include:

- Tax information
- Employment records
- Your lease or mortgage records
- Insurance records
- Bank records and other financial information
- Important projects, both work-related and personal
- Software you purchased and installed from the Internet
- Computer scheduling programme such as Microsoft Outlook
- Digital photographs that are important to you
- Music files you do not want to lose
- Your e-mail address book
- Your Internet bookmarks

It is not generally considered necessary to back-up software such as word processing or spreadsheet programmes. If your computer is attacked or crashes due to other reasons, you can easily reinstall the software on a new computer and reset any preferences. Backing-up these programmes will take up a huge amount of space on a CD or zip drive. Even if the software disks are lost, you should be able to get them replaced.

Although you may have important files on your home computer, your back-up needs will be different if you operate a business out of your home.

In that case, you will need to identify what business information is irreplaceable.

The Solutions

Select a secure location for back-up copies, whether paper or digital. At the very least this should be a different location–away from your business or home–from where the originals are stored and used. The storage space should be as secure as possible–at least locked and hidden–and should also be fire or water resistant.

As you consider storage options, do not forget one of the most traditional solutions–a safe deposit box. Your financial institution probably offers a safe deposit box service for a small fee. Once you acquire the box, you are issued a key to it. The box cannot be opened by anybody who does not have that key. In most cases, financial institutions will ask for your identification before you can access your own safe deposit box. The contents are private, and the staff of the financial institution will not be physically present when you either remove or add an item to the box. You can use a safe deposit box to store computer CDs as well as paper items and valuables.

Unless absolutely necessary, do not ask family or friends to store copies of your files–either paper or computer. It is unfortunate, but even people you believe are trustworthy can steal your information or be careless about their storage of it.

If you are an occasional user, weekly back-up may be sufficient. If you are a heavy computer user or use your computer for a home-based business, you may want to back-up on a daily basis. Another approach is to consider how often the files are changed. For example, if your files are changed daily, you should back-up the files on a daily basis; if updated weekly, back-up on a weekly basis and so on. Either way, label the back-up disks carefully, and do not erase the previous back-up until you make a new one and determine the back-up was effective.

Make a checklist of what files you wish to save and their order of priority. A general rule is that any file–hard copy or computer–that cannot easily be replaced should be at the top of the list.

You should schedule time to back-up your files just the way you would schedule any important task. It is easy to push aside a back-up chore when it seems other things are more important, but it is necessary to do this on a regular basis. You might consider doing the back-up at the end of the day or your work week as a way to finish your work.

In the case of important computer files, consider using both an electronic back-up–such as a removable CD–and a printout. In the worst case scenario that you lose your computer hard drive and your back-up CDs, you will at least have a way to recreate the document.

When you back-up computer files make sure the copy and transfer of the information is successful. Depending on the back-up media you use, a mechanical glitch can result in the information not being able to be accessed when you need it.

There are four major methods of backing-up you computer files. Which one you use depends on the type of equipment you are using and how comfortable you are with the back-up medium.

- **Hard disks**. Hard disks used to be the medium of choice to download software, transfer files and back-up files. All you have to do to back-up files to a hard disk is to use the copy function of your software or click and drag the file to the disk. The disadvantages of floppy disks are that they do not have much storage capacity–usually up to 1.44 MB of data–and many newer computers do not have floppy disk drives.

- **CD writers.** As compared to a hard disk, a CD can carry up to 800 MB of data. They are the standard now for downloading software, and virtually all computers have CD drives or can handle an external CD drive. The back-up process is similar to that of a floppy disk.

- **ZIP drives.** These drives are not used as much as they were for back-up, but they are still a popular and simple way to back-up information. You will probably have to purchase an external ZIP drive for your computer.

- **Thumb or Travel, flash drives or memory sticks.** These are highly portable devices that can be plugged into a computer quickly, from which the files can be downloaded and then either be stored or used to transfer the information to another computer. The amount of space available on a thumb drive varies from drive to drive. They can hold anywhere from 1 GB to 120 GB.

If you prefer, you can also buy software back-up programmes that will help you back-up your most important files. In most cases, this software is relatively inexpensive and very simple to use.

One method of backing-up your paper files is to have them scanned onto a CD. This CD can be accessed from a computer and your files can be printed. You will probably want to make two copies of this CD and keep them with your important files.

Backing-up important hard-copy documents may mean visiting a commercial copying center and copying the paper files. It is important you do not store these copied paper files with the original, because any loss of the original will surely result in a loss of your copies. Keep the copies in a different location that is as secure as possible and less likely to be destroyed by fire or flood. Be careful not to leave any original files or copies at the copy center.

Active Duty Alerts for Military Personnel

By the nature of their duties, military personnel are often extremely vulnerable to identity theft, especially when they are stationed outside the country.

Military personnel have to rely more on online and phone services to check on credit card accounts and financial accounts, a process that can expose them to the risk of identity theft. Also, fraudsters who are aware of the duty status of military personnel may specifically target them for identity theft, because their being out of the country makes it difficult to keep up with financial affairs generally and to detect identity theft in particular.

If you are a member of the military or a family member of a member of the armed forces, you should be aware of the danger of identity theft for military personnel, how to file an active duty alert and how the alert helps prevent identity theft.

This alert serves as protection for those deployed in locations or situations in which they are unlikely to be able to apply for credit or monitor their financial accounts.

Most cases of identity theft of military personnel occur when the serviceperson is stationed outside the country and away from his or her base. These military personnel may not pay as close attention to their financial accounts while they are away from home.

The three major credit reporting bureaus will place active duty fraud alerts on your accounts if you properly request them. The alerts last 1 year. If your tour of duty extends beyond 1 year, you can place another alert on your credit report. This service should be provided at no charge to you.

When businesses see an active duty alert on your credit reports, they are required to verify your identity before issuing any new credit under your name.

In the case of full-time or reserve military personnel, a call-up to active duty outside the United Kingdom will mean major, and, in many cases, unexpected disruption of their lives. On short notice, they must make arrangements:

- With their regular employers regarding how to handle their work while they are gone;
- with their immediate family for handling domestic duties that would normally be their responsibility. These responsibilities might include paying bills and monitoring financial activities; and

- with their family and friends to develop new lines of communications, such as phone trees and blogs.

All of these pressures may result in military personnel not being as diligent as they should be regarding their identity.

The Internet has been a boon for military personnel stationed outside the United Kingdom to communicate with friends and family and to conduct business online. However, frequently military personnel are not as careful as they should be in what they communicate via e-mail and what information they supply online. Remember, e-mail is never a secure way to transmit any financial or personal identification information.

When you place an active duty alert on your credit reports, you will be automatically removed from the credit reporting companies' marketing lists. These lists are used by credit card companies to solicit new credit accounts. If this mail were sent to you when you were not at home or at your base, it could be intercepted easily by fraudsters.

Just placing an active duty alert on your credit reports will not protect you from all forms of identity theft. It will primarily protect you from a fraudster opening new credit accounts in your name. An active duty alert will do little to protect you from other types of identity theft, such as the theft of your

National Insurance number or someone gaining access to your financial accounts.

The Solutions

Be very careful about who you ask to take care of your financial issues while you are on active duty outside the UK. Unfortunately, most cases of identity theft are committed by a family member or friend who appropriates your identity to help with their own financial problems, such as inability to get new credit or pay bills.

If you do request someone besides a spouse to take care of your financial accounts while you are on duty outside the United States, make sure you have ways to hold that person accountable. Ask that person to send you regular reports on what he or she has done and why. This can be done via e-mail.

You will probably have to place an active duty alert on your reports by sending letters to the credit bureaus, preferably by certified mail or the available equivalent. In your letter, include appropriate proof of your identity, including:

- Your legal name as it appears on your military records
- Your current address
- Your National Insurance number

You do not need to contact each of the three credit reporting bureaus to place an active duty alert on your accounts. Similar to placing an initial fraud alert, if you place an active duty alert with one credit reporting bureau, the other two should add the alert to their reports. The same applies if you remove the alert from your report.

After you have placed the request with the credit bureaus and know it has been received, obtain a copy of your current credit report and make sure it contains the active duty alert you requested.

If you apply for new credit while you are on active duty and have placed an active duty alert on your credit reports, make sure any creditor you have submitted an application to has your most current contact information. If you do not do this, the business may be unable to make the necessary confirmation and so you may experience delays in opening new credit.

An active duty alert will remove your name from credit bureau marketing lists for 2 years. However, you can ask to be put back on the list before that period is over.

You do not necessarily have to place an active duty alert on your account yourself. If you are in a situation that does not allow you to do this, you can designate a personal representative who can send the information to the credit bureau for you. Also ask them to follow up in the same way that you would: by requesting a copy of your report to confirm that the alert appears there. There are some commercial services that can help you with the process, but the cost may not justify using them. You can select a reliable person yourself.

Credit Monitoring Services

Many consumers consider using a credit monitoring service to free themselves from the work of maintaining constant vigilance on their accounts. However, this service does have costs attached and while it may save you some time and effort, it may not be worth the investment. You must understand what you can do yourself to monitor your credit, what a credit monitoring service can do for you and whether using such a service is right for you.

There are specific items most credit monitoring services will be looking for on your credit reports.

- Inquiries to your credit file
- New account activity
- Address changes indicating a fraudster has changed a mailing address so a statement will be sent to them

- Accounts that have been referred to a collection agency
- Changes to account information
- Credit limit increases
- Changes to public records that would include judgments and bankruptcies
- Changes to existing accounts
- Closed accounts

Credit monitoring services, while possibly expensive, can offer some valuable services to you, especially if you have already been a victim of identity theft.

- Credit monitoring services may provide early detection of errors or suspicious activity.
- Some services will provide fraud resolution services that might help you in fixing the problems related to identity theft.
- Credit monitoring services may offer identity theft insurance, although the value of this insurance is not always worth the cost.

No matter what claims it may make, there are definite limitations to what a credit monitoring service can provide you.

- Many services will only monitor one credit reporting bureau, which may prevent you from learning about clues to a fraud that would have showed up on the reports of the other two bureaus. For example, perhaps you use a service that only monitors the

Callcredit credit bureau. If a fraudster attempts to make a large purchase and the retailer pulls a credit report from the Experian credit bureau, your credit monitoring service will not send you an alert about the request for your credit report because it doesn't even know it has taken place.

- The monitoring may not be timely. Ideally, a credit monitoring service will send you alerts within 24 hours of detecting them.

- Credit reporting services can be costly, with services offering daily monitoring averaging $100 per year.

Most credit monitoring services will advertise their product as privacy protection or anti-ID-theft services. However, monitoring a credit report is not a deterrent to identity theft. It is a way to detect theft that has already occurred.

All three credit reporting bureaus offer credit monitoring services, usually promoted on their Websites. There are also private monitoring services that will monitor all three credit bureaus. There are three credit monitoring services that are rated highly by Fight Identity Theft.

- Identity Watch™ www.econsumer.equifax.co.uk
- Privacy Guard www.privacyguard.co.uk
- Credit Expert Monitoring from Experian www.creditexpert.co.uk

Unlike credit management services or credit repair services for people with real debt problems, using a credit monitoring service will not have a negative affect on your credit score.

Whether you request your credit report or have it done by a credit monitoring service, it will appear on your credit report as a consumer pull. This is an important designation, because a large number of requests on your credit report–from which someone might infer that you are requesting new credit–can negatively affect your credit rating.

The Solutions

The people who benefit most from signing up to a credit monitoring service are those who have been victims of identity theft, or believe–based on actions such as losing a wallet or being the victim of a home burglary–they may become victims of identity theft. Most other consumers are probably fine reviewing their own credit reports, as long as they do it at least once a year.

Whether you use a credit monitoring service or decide to do it yourself, you should consider getting more than one copy of your report every year, perhaps at least one every quarter. The credit reporting bureaus will gladly sell you extra copies of your report, or, for a fee, allow you online access, so you can review the report at any time.

Expect an order form for a credit monitoring service to ask for a lot of information about you. However, this information is necessary to verify your identity and keep it secure. If you feel uncomfortable providing this type of information, consider checking your credit report yourself.

If you decide to use a credit monitoring service, you might consider one that monitors all three credit bureaus and not just one of them. Also, when you are reviewing your credit monitoring service options, take a close look at how often the monitoring service checks its client's reports. In some cases, the interval between checks is long, which means you will not be alerted to possible identity theft until the damage has been going on for a long time. Also determine if the service will provide you with regular credit updates or just alerts based on activities possibly related to identity theft. General updates can be useful in other ways, namely so that at any given time you know what your credit situation is.

If you decide to purchase additional fraud resolution services or identity theft insurance from a credit monitoring service, be very careful about what you are purchasing. As with the actual monitoring, you can do most of the fraud resolution yourself without spending the extra money. Make sure the identity theft insurance covers the major costs of combating an identity theft, such as lost wages, postage, travel, and legal expenses and photocopying costs. The insurance should have a low deductible and not cost more than $25 to $40 per year.

Pay attention to what your credit monitoring service is sending you even if it is not an alert. The fact is most people will use a credit monitoring service extensively when they first sign up and then lose interest. If it is worth the money to sign up for a service, it is worth your time to pay attention to what the service is sending you.

Just as you would for any important service or product you are considering purchasing, you need to do your research before you choose a credit monitoring service. If you select the service offered by one of the three major credit reporting bureaus, you will be using a reputable company. If you are investigating another company make sure you know the facts.

- What the service will cost.
- What items on your credit report will be monitored.
- How often your credit report will be reviewed.
- How quickly you will receive an alert to any suspicious activity.
- Whether they will provide you with copies of your credit report and not just alerts.

Part 4

LEARN WHO TO CONTACT IF SOMETHING GOES WRONG

■■■

Becoming a victim of identity theft means you will be spending a significant amount of time dealing with the crime, especially time spent contacting the various companies that are affected by the theft.

But, you will also need to work with government agencies and other organisations to make sure the crime is properly reported and addressed. Most of these agencies and organisations will try hard to work with you and make the process as painless as possible, but you can still expect to spend quite a lot of time reporting the crime and then following up. By reporting the crime, you are not only alerting law enforcement and government agencies to the crime that was committed against you but giving them the opportunity to use these facts possibly to catch the criminal and prevent other crimes from taking place.

Later in this chapter, you will be given specific information on how to contact the major agencies and organisations you will need to report your identity theft to. The information below will help you sort out who is worth contacting and who is not.

The best way to proceed in making the proper notifications is to do your research by visiting the Direct.gov.uk or Homeoffice.gov.uk Websites, among others. They will have the information you need to contact the proper authorities.

Expect to be met with skepticism by those working for some of the agencies and organisations you contact. These people want to work on correcting the problem of identity theft but on a daily basis they will have people contact them who are really not identity theft victims but rather are just misinterpreting activity they have done themselves. Do not give up on the contact simply because the person you are talking to asks you a lot of questions.

Besides notifying the proper authorities, there are other organisations and companies that will want to know what has happened to you. This information–

without making a specific reference to you–will alert others to the type of fraud that you have been a victim of and also help the organisations compile data and conduct research on identity theft.

The Solutions

You will probably have to make your complaint in writing and provide documentation–such as copies of credit reports or financial statements–to help substantiate that what you are reporting really happened.

When you talk to somebody on the telephone, keep records of whom you spoke with and what was discussed. When you finish the call, be sure to inquire if there is any other office or agency you should inform.

The major governmental agencies listed below all have different areas of responsibility, so you will report the crime to different ones depending on the nature of the theft against you.

- **Consumer Direct** is the major governmental clearinghouse for reporting identity theft. They may not provide any specific help for you, but they will value the information you provide. Telephone: 08454 04 05 06.

- **Department of Homeland Security** operates a computer security service called the National Cyber Security Division. This agency's mission is to work with other agencies and companies to maintain security in cyberspace. If you believe you are a victim of online fraud, you should contact them.

- **Royal Mail** goes after criminals who use the mail to commit their crimes. Much of identity theft involves the fraudulent interception of mail or sending out fraudulent requests for information through the mail. Often, mail fraud charges are used to arrest and convict criminals engaging in other activity that is harder to prove.

- **OFT (Office of Fair Trading)** offers sound advice to identifying and beating scammers. Telephone: 08457 22 44 99.

- **FSA (Financial Services Authority)** to report investment scams. Telephone: 0845 606 1234 or www.fsa.gov.uk.

- Banksafeonline.org.uk works to protect bank customers from phishing scams. Forward any suspected emails to reports@banksafeonline.org.uk and they will investigate and track down the perpetrators.

- **DVLA (Driver & Vehicle Licensing Agency)** should be alerted if you believe someone has stolen your driver's licence or is using your identity information to establish a false driver's licence www.dvla.gov.uk.

- **HomeOffice** offers general information and advice on fraud and how to protect yourself from becoming a victim. The fraud information page is www.homeoffice.gov.uk/crime-victims/reducing-crime/fraud.

Learn Who to Contact if Something Goes Wrong 205

- **The Fraud Reduction Website** is published by the National Working Group on Fraud on behalf of the UK Association of Chief Police Officers (ACPO) and offers advice on how to respond to suspected frauds against business www.acpo.police.uk.
- **IPS (Identity & Passport Service)** to report if your passport or ID card has been stolen or you think your identity has been stolen or used fraudulently.
- **CIFAS Protective Registration Service** (operated by Equifax) is the UK's Fraud Preventing Service as a member association dedicated to the prevention of financial crime.www.cifas.org.uk.

Your local law authorities should be alerted to the theft. This includes a municipal police department or sheriff's department, depending on the type of community you live in. Make sure you get a copy of the police report to use as proof of the crime; you may need it in order to file other reports.

The British embassy needs to be contacted immediately if you are travelling abroad and your passport is stolen.

Besides the governmental agencies interested in your identity theft, there are also several companies and other organisations that want to know about your theft.

- **Citizens Advice Bureau** – see local telephone directory or www.citizensadvice.org.uk.
- **Consumer Direct** – www.consumerdirect.gov.uk/watch_out/scams.

- **Crimestoppers** – 0800 555111 or www.crimestoppers-uk.org.
- **National Identity Fraud Prevention Week** – www.stop-idfraud.co.uk.
- **Police Fraud Squads** – see your local telephone directory.
- **Trading Standards** (for consumer protection) – see your local telephone directory or www.trading-standards.gov.uk.

Consumer credit reporting bureaus will want you to alert them immediately if you detect any unauthorised activity on your credit accounts and will help you file a fraud alert on the reports. Contact:

CallCredit, Ltd.
Consumer Services Team
P.O. Box 491
Leeds   LS3 1WX
t. 0870 060 1414
www.callcredit.co.uk

Equifax, PLC
P.O. Box 1140
Bradford BD1 54S
t. 0870 010 0583
www.equifax.co.uk

Experian, Ltd.
P.O. Box 9000
Nottingham NG80 7WP
t. 0870 241 6212
www.experian.co.uk

Do not ignore your local media. If you believe you have been victimized by identity theft, especially in an unusual manner, call the newsrooms of your local media and report the story. They may decide to do nothing about it, but, depending on the nature of the story, they may print or broadcast it and help others to avoid what happened to you.

Talking to the Right People

Your communication skills are going to be tested if you are the victim of identity theft. You will need to be in touch with law enforcement agents as well as representatives from the credit reporting bureaus and your credit card companies and financial institutions. In all these cases, by making sure you are always talking to someone who can take action on your concern, you will save yourself a lot of time and stress.

Reporting requirements vary with the type of fraud detected and the amount of loss incurred. It is important that you know what information each party will need and how best to communicate that information in order to remedy the situation.

Dealing with a phone tree or voice-mail system is frustrating because it feels like you are being prevented from speaking with a real person. But remember that phone trees and voice-mail systems are simply tools that companies use to direct calls to the proper staff person.

Often it will seem like the person you are speaking with on the phone is discounting the importance of your call, has had minimal training in dealing with your situation or is not even actually in-country but rather somewhere in another country. In any of these situations, do not allow yourself to become frustrated. Indulging your feelings of frustration will only distract you from the important business at hand. And there is no substitute for talking to a real person. Simply leaving a message or using e-mail is not the way to communicate effectively your concerns over a possible identity theft.

An institution does have to reply to your concerns. When you talk to a person regarding your identity theft, you need to know they are aware of this responsibility and what they need to do to help.

There is more to reporting identity theft than simply reporting it to a company affected by the theft. A very important part of combating the identity theft against you is to make contact with the major credit reporting bureaus and alert them to the possibility that your identity has been compromised. Online services are also very interested in any misuse of their names or services. Most online shopping services or auction Websites will offer a means to report any suspected identity theft. Also, federal and state agencies have phone and online services designed to receive complaints about identity theft.

The Solutions

If you believe your identity has been compromised, there are numerous companies and organisations that should be on the top of your list to call. Depending on the nature of the crime, they may include:

- Your credit card companies
- Your financial institutions
- Telephone companies
- Royal Mail
- The three major credit bureaus (Callcredit, Experian, Equifax)
- Debt collectors
- Law enforcement agencies including local and national government agencies

It is important to report identity theft as soon as you think you have been victimized. Be prepared to work your way through a phone tree system and leave many voice mail messages before you have an actual contact: A conversation with a real person who is qualified to assist with your identity theft-related issues.

Remember your rights as you make your phone calls. You have a right to obtain documents regarding any fraudulent activity on your accounts, you have a right to obtain information from a debt collector, you have the right to request that fraudulent information be removed from your credit report and you have the right to request businesses do not report information about you to consumer reporting agencies if you believe this information is based on identity theft. With each company or organisation you contact, make sure you are speaking with a person who can act on these rights.

Sometimes you will need to talk directly to a merchant and not just a credit card company. For example, if a merchant has rejected your cheque, you need to be able to explain to him or her what has happened to you and exchange specific information that will lead to your cheque being accepted. In such a situation, make sure the person you are talking with actually has the authority to address the issue. Especially in the cases of small businesses, it is usually the owner who will have the authority to properly address your issues.

When you call one of the major credit bureaus to report identity theft, the information should be sent to the other credit bureaus. You need to make sure that the person you are speaking with understands the need to pass the alert along to the other bureaus.

Learn Who to Contact if Something Goes Wrong 211

Keep your composure when you are talking to a law enforcement investigator. You are upset about that has happened to you, and you have probably had little contact with legal authorities. It may seem like the person you are talking to may not appear to care about your situation, but they will do their job to help you. Expect that it may take a few days for a law enforcement officer to return your call and discuss the details of your case.

Try to remember you are dealing with a person and not a machine. Often a sense of humor or the ability to keep this problem in perspective will help you make progress with someone who does not seem to care about your situation.

Stay focused and do not be tempted to ramble. The person you are talking with probably wants to do his or her job but does not need to know any more from you than necessary.

Remember your identity may have been misappropriated to set-up fraudulent phone accounts–either landlines or cell phones–in your name. If you believe your identity has been compromised in this way, contact your phone companies to make sure they are aware of the possibility of fraud on your accounts.

Expect that you will probably have to make an initial contact with a letter and then follow up with a phone call. The communication process may be made easier by putting some type of identification code on the letter referring to your case.

Do not give up trying to find the right person who can help you resolve your situation. Keep asking the important questions, and do not let yourself get dismissed from a call. Just because someone says they are a manager does not mean they have any more authority than the first person you spoke to.

Keep a journal with notes detailing whom you have discussed this case with and what each person you have spoken to has said they will do. Allow a reasonable amount of time for them to take that action, and then do not hesitate to call back and ask for that person if you believe the action has not taken place.

Identity Theft Complaints and Notices

Paperwork will occupy a large part of your effort to combat the damage of having your identity stolen. You will have to notify the three credit reporting bureaus in writing, file a report with your local law enforcement agencies and complete an Identity Theft Affidavit.

Learn Who to Contact if Something Goes Wrong   213

In addition, you will have to file individual complaints and notices regarding the fraudulent use of your identity to the companies that have been affected by the crime. This means you must know what each company will want to receive from you, how to clearly state your complaint and what you must do to follow up after you have filed the complaint or given notice to the company.

A complaint form, letter or notice you send to an individual business is not the same as a fraud alert. Fraud alerts are filed with the three major credit reporting bureaus, which will place the alert on your credit report. This will alert any business checking your report that you have been the victim of identity theft and therefore activities conducted in your name, such as an attempt to open a new account, could be fraudulent.

You must be prepared to include as detailed information as possible on any complaint form or notice.

- Your name, address and NI number;
- the account number affected;
- the date(s) when you believe your identity was stolen;
- the exact transactions and the amount of money involved in each; and
- any information about who might have stolen your identity and made the transactions.

When you file a complaint form or notice with a business, the burden is on you to prove that the crime has occurred. The burden of proof lies with the victim because some unscrupulous people will dispute transactions they have actually made–claiming they were the result of identity theft–so they can avoid paying for the transaction.

Any company must provide you with a copy of an account application or list of account activities relating to your identity theft if you request it in writing. When you request a copy of your records for the purpose of filing a complaint or notice, the company will probably ask for additional information before they send you the information.

- Proof of your identity that may be a photocopy of a government issued ID, such as a driver's licence, passport or other official ID, and
- a police report and a completed affidavit which may be the Identity Theft Affidavit or the company's individual affidavit.

The company must provide you with this information at no charge within 30 days of receiving your request and supporting documents. When you receive them, share them immediately with law enforcement. This can help expedite their investigation and bring the criminal to justice.

In the case of resolving a dispute with a financial institution by filing a complaint or notice, the institution generally has 10 business days to investigate the complaint. The institution must then tell you the results of the investigation within 3 working days of completing it. Any confirmed error must be corrected within 1 business day after the institution has determined it did occur. If the institution needs a longer period to investigate, it can take up to 45 days providing it replaces the disputed funds to your account.

The Solutions

To dispute charges and debits on your existing account that you believe were not made by you, request a copy of the company's fraud dispute form. The also has a form you can use as a template to create your own letter. However you decide to make the complaint, make sure you send it to the business' billing inquiries address and not the address you use for sending your payments.

After you have resolved the disputed activities on your account, request the company send you a letter stating the dispute has been resolved and what the company did to clean your record. Keep these letters with the rest of your paperwork pertaining to your identity theft.

Providing proof of your identity theft–such as actual fraudulent application forms–may help you further your case with law enforcement. The forms may contain evidence such as an obviously forged signature or an incorrect address.

You will probably have to submit more than just a complaint form or written notice to get a business to correct any illegal activity on your accounts. Many companies will ask for supporting information such as an Identity Theft Affidavit, a notated record of your transactions and, possibly, a written police report.

In almost all cases of disputing identity theft, you will have to submit all information in writing. For security reasons, businesses do not usually want this information transmitted online or by phone.

Send your complaint letter and supporting documentation to a credit card company within 60 days after the statement containing the suspicious information was sent to you. If the actions of a fraudster results in you not getting your bill, you should report the suspected activities within 60 days of when you would normally receive it.

Always send your complaint letter and supporting documents by certified mail so you can receive a receipt indicating that the business received your information.

As part of your complaint and, if the activity is occurring on existing accounts, you should request

Learn Who to Contact if Something Goes Wrong 217

the company send you replacement cards with new account numbers. Ask that the old accounts be processed as account closed at consumer's request, not that the card was lost or stolen.

Your complaint letter to the business should request they do not submit the disputed information to the credit reporting bureaus. You will need to be very specific about what information you do not want reported and will probably have to file a police identity theft report.

At some point, you may have to deal with a debt collection agency that is attempting to collect on a debt you did not incur. You can use methods similar to commercial business complaint forms to halt the collection activities.

- Write a dispute letter to the agency requesting they stop collection activities. Once your letter is received, the agency cannot contact you again except to tell you there will be no further contact or what specific action they or the creditor will take next.
- You have 30 days from the receipt of the disputed collection attempt to write the agency. Attach supporting documents, such as a police report, to your dispute letter to substantiate your claim.

Closing Compromised Accounts

Identity theft can affect a variety of your accounts. These can include your credit cards and financial accounts, phone services, ISP providers and cable providers. Your first reaction after you discover misuse of your accounts through identity theft might be to immediately close the affected accounts. But, this can end up causing as much trouble as it might solve and prove to be very difficult to do. The difficulty factor is even higher if you are closing accounts that you did not open. You need to know what accounts should be closed, what criteria to use to decide to close the account and what you can expect from the process.

There are many accounts that can be affected by identity theft.

- Credit card accounts
- Financial institution accounts
- Phone accounts
- ISP accounts

Expect the process of closing an account to take a little time and effort. And although you might find this frustrating, remember that it is also for your benefit: You would not want the process to be so easy that just anyone could close one of your accounts.

There may be more involved in dealing with an account that has had fraudulent activity on it than merely closing the account. You should be prepared to dispute specific unauthorised charges or activities that have affected your account. Remember, most credit card companies will limit your liabilities once you have reported the unauthorised use of the accounts due to identity theft.

Closing an account–whether it is a financial account or a credit card–is usually not accomplished immediately; each company has its own procedure, and the amount of time it takes to close one account may be quite different from the amount it takes to close another. Also note that you will probably have to wait some time before you can open a new account with the same company. Depending on how you use the account, this could be a major inconvenience.

Most credit card bills will include information on what you need to do to close the account. This information frequently appears in the fine print on the back of the document that is mostly boiler-plate language. You need to review the requirements on reporting fraud and closing accounts carefully before you take action. If you do not see this information on your monthly bills, check the company's Website.

Part of the process of closing accounts that were falsely established in your name may involve you asking for copies of any of the forms sent to the company to establish the account. The company will supply you with this information if you send them proof of your identification and a police report. This record may have information that will be helpful in your local police investigate the crime.

Fraudulent activity on your credit card may not be noticed by you until a debt collection agency contacts you. Request the agency's fraud affidavit form and clearly indicate what activity is unauthorised by you and if you have closed the account.

It is possible that any fraudulent activity on your account has already been listed on your credit report. You can discover that information by carefully reviewing your credit reports. It will still be your responsibility to refute this fraudulent information with the credit reporting bureaus. Merely disputing the activity with your credit card companies will not necessarily remove this information from your credit reports.

The Solutions

Carefully consider whether you wish to close an account. Even though there may have been illegal activity in the account, it might be better to simply alert the credit card company or financial institution about the theft and not completely close the account.

Learn Who to Contact if Something Goes Wrong   221

Most credit card companies and financial institutions do not want to go through the effort of closing an account. The person you speak to may have other suggestions besides closing the account. Consider these suggestions carefully and decide if they are really in your best interest or are options that are better for the institution.

To close an account with most credit card companies and financial institutions you will first have to call and speak to someone in the fraud or security department of the company. Just speaking to a customer service representative–or using e-mail–will not be enough. During this telephone call, get the exact name of the person you are speaking with and get detailed information about exactly what the company will need to receive from you to close your account.

Next, you will follow up on your initial phone call in writing with the appropriate individual in the fraud or security division of the company. Make sure you include or attach all of the information and materials that your contact told you were necessary. Send your written correspondence by return receipt mail or using a shipping company that requires the recipient to sign for the envelope. Having this receipt or other proof will help if at any point the company claims it never received your correspondence.

If you are disputing specific unauthorised charges on your account as well as closing the account, there are certain things you should ask the company to do.

- If the charges or debits are on existing accounts, ask the fraud or security person to send you the company's fraud dispute forms.

- If the company does not have any dispute forms, be prepared to write your own letter to dispute the charges and be prepared to provide proof that your identity was stolen. This proof, in many cases, may include a police report regarding the identity theft.

- Whether you send back a company-generated dispute form or your own letter, be sure to send the information to the address from the company regarding billing inquiries and not the address for sending payments on your account.

When you request a compromised account be closed, you should ask that the activity be listed as account closed at consumer's request. If the activity is reported as card lost or stolen, it could be misrepresented as blaming you and prevent you from receiving new credit.

If you decide to open a new account after you have closed the compromised account, be sure to establish new user IDs and PINs that will be difficult for a fraudster to access. Consider using a random series of letters and numbers rather than some easily

Learn Who to Contact if Something Goes Wrong

identified information such as your birthday, your mother's maiden name or the last four digits of your NI number.

If you discover new and unauthorised accounts opened in your name-usually discovered by reviewing your credit reports-ask if the credit bureau will accept a standard ID theft affidavit. If they will not, ask the bureau to send you their specific fraud dispute form.

Start an identity theft correspondence file, and keep copies of all relevant correspondence with your credit card companies and financial institutions-both from you and from the company-in it. Every time you make contact by telephone regarding your account, note the name of the person you spoke with and the date and time of the contact. Have both your correspondence file and your phone log in front of you whenever you make a call, because often you will not speak with the same person twice.

After you have resolved the credit dispute with a company by successfully closing your accounts, request a letter stating you have closed the accounts and successfully discharged any fraudulent charges that may have appeared on the account. This will be a major part of your proof that your account is cleared and closed in the event that any other fraudulent activities are made on the account.

Disputing fraudulent activity on your credit card, reporting a lost or stolen card or requesting an account be closed will be easier if you took some preventive measures before the theft occurred. The most important is to keep a copy of all your credit card and financial account numbers in a secure place that only you have access to.

As with many aspects of fighting identity theft, you need to be persistent and consistent in your approach. If you believe you are not getting the response you want from a fraud or security representative, request to speak to a supervisor or manager. Make sure you always refer to the same information–especially a police report number–every time you contact the credit card company or financial institution.

Filing a Police Report

If your home has been burglarised or you have been a victim of a pickpocket, report the crime immediately. This crime may not result in a case of identity theft against you, but the police will still want to be aware of the details of the crime. At this point, you will need to remain vigilant to the possibility of identity theft–and the possibility of needing to file a second police report. Before filing the identity theft report,

Learn Who to Contact if Something Goes Wrong

make a rough draft of your story and outline, in chronological order, what happened to you and why you believe your identity has been stolen. Use your identity theft journal and notes to help prepare your rough draft. Include the following information:

- How you first discovered the theft (including who told you and under what circumstances).
- The contact information for any company you have contacted regarding the theft, including the names and phone numbers.
- The full and accurate account numbers for all accounts affected by the fraudster;
- The locations where fraudulent uses of existing accounts or applications for new accounts occurred.
- The names, addresses and telephone numbers listed on false credit applications.
- Any other information that might provide clues about the possible fraudster.
- Copies of any correspondence or account statements involved in your discovery of the theft.

When you report your theft to the police, be sure to bring as much documentation as you can to prove the theft has occurred. Documentation might include:

- Debt collection letters
- Credit reports

Make sure you keep a copy of the police report in your journal regarding your identity theft. It may be necessary to use it to report the theft to the companies affected by it. Always keep a copy and simply make additional copies as needed.

If you run into reluctance from your local police to take your report of identity theft, you may be able to file a report as a miscellaneous incidents report. You can also consider trying another jurisdiction, such as your state police. You can also check with your state attorney general's office to find out if your police are required to take an identity theft report.

Do not give up if your local police tell you they cannot take a report. Remind them you need the report for your creditors to resolve the fraud that has occurred and you will also need the report to place a long-term fraud alert on your credit reports.

Filing a police report is not a cure-all for identity theft. You will still have to go through the effort of contacting the credit reporting bureaus, your credit card companies and your financial institutions. Do not expect the police to do this for you; this responsibility will fall to you.

You may feel reluctant to report the crime if you believe the identity theft was committed by a family member, friend or co-worker. Remember that you do not have to press charges, but you will still need to file a police report because many of the affected companies will require it.

If your case is assigned a specific investigator, make sure you get the name of the investigator and his or her contact phone number. Supply it with a copy of your police report to any companies affected by the theft so they can call and verify the theft has been properly reported.

If other criminal activities have occurred using your name and that perpetrator has been arrested, be sure to contact immediately the law enforcement agency and file an impersonation report with the agency. This may require you to give your fingerprints and have your photo taken to verify your identity. Make sure the police compare your information with the fingerprints and photo of the perpetrator. Ask the law enforcement agency to send the false identity claim to the local district attorney's office.

Once your name is placed on a criminal database, even if it was because of your identity being used in a crime, it is unlikely it will ever be completely removed. Therefore, request that your local law enforcement agency change the key name or primary name on the report to John Doe and that your name be listed as an alias.

Organising Your Case Notes

One of the most frustrating parts of being a victim of identity theft is the effort you will have to make to report and correct the crimes. Law enforcement officials, credit card companies and financial institutions will offer as much help as possible, but, ultimately it will be your responsibility to follow the case to a satisfying conclusion.

Identity theft victims frequently find themselves feeling helpless. They feel as though an important part of their lives has been compromised. This feeling of helplessness can sometimes limit a person's ability to logically deal with the problem.

However, it is vital that you look at the problem logically and design a system for keeping your records and reports organised. Time spent organizing at the beginning of the process will pay off in reduced time and stress correcting the problem.

The effects of identity theft can last for a long time, no matter how hard you work to resolve the issues. The best way to deal with the long-term effects are to keep careful records of what you have done and what responses resulted.

Initially you may be confused about which governmental agencies, organisations and companies you should report your identity theft to. There will probably be at least four parts of reporting your identity theft:

- Reports with all the companies affected by the theft;
- a report to at least one credit reporting bureau (with the instruction that that bureau should inform the others);
- a report with the appropriate local or government agency; and
- keeping detailed records. Your records of your contacts are absolutely invaluable in managing how you respond to identity theft. The records will allow you to know when you discovered the theft, what actions you have taken and who you have contacted either in writing, by phone or by e-mail.

It does work to file complaints with the proper authorities. Government agencies and organisations do want to know about these crimes so they can pass the information along to others. It may seem like there are too many steps and organisations to keep track of and that surely some of them are unimportant, but this is not true.

A journal of your activities will not only help you keep track of your activities, but it will also help you keep track of your time and the expenses you have incurred in dealing with the case and help you prove what financial restitution you should expect should the crime be solved.

The Solutions

Try to think like a police officer or lawyer when you are organizing your notes. You must keep your records current, and they should be easy to understand.

Just as you should protect your identity, you need to protect the files and notes you are keeping on how you are dealing with the identity theft. Make sure they are stored in a secure location in your home such as a locked drawer or safe.

Use basic office tools to keep your information organised, and do not just let papers pile up on your desk. Consider using a simple three-ring binder, and put all documents and notes into the binder as soon as you realise they are relevant to your identity theft case.

There are several ways to organise your notes to help you deal with the legal and financial institutions that will help resolve your problem.

- Keep a dated case log either on computer or paper. Avoid the temptation to keep information on sticky notes and instead, enter it directly into the log. You can always refine it later.

- Keep track of everyone you speak with in a telephone log. (You may want to incorporate this information into your case log). Make sure the information you enter includes the contact information of the person you spoke with, the date and time of the contact and

Learn Who to Contact if Something Goes Wrong

the information you gathered. Also clearly indicate what the next step is and who needs to take it–you or the person you spoke with.

- Send a confirmation of agreements and discussions after you have made a contact and discussed your case. This confirmation should include some mechanism for the person you have contacted to agree this is what was discussed. In some cases, the institution you deal with may be willing to send you a confirmation, but you should be prepared to do it yourself.

- A log of items that you have received by mail. Include information about who sent each item and what you did with it.

- Maintain an expense list of all costs incurred while working to remedy the crime, including phone calls, postage, mileage, legal costs, notary fees, court costs, lost time from work and any materials you purchase. Some of these costs may be reimbursable.

- If your case goes to court, attend the trial and take notes on what is done. Make sure the notes include the name of the judge and the attorneys involved in the case.

- Keep a copy of any official records such as police reports.

- Make sure you keep a copy of all the physical proof of the fraud–for instance, credit reports, financial reports and phone records–as part of your records.

- File copies of any letters you send or replies you receive regarding your case.

Below is a list of some fixed costs related to remedying some problems caused by your identity theft.

- If your National Insurance number has been stolen, you will not have to pay anything to correct the problem and you can request a new number.
- If your driver's licence has been stolen, you may have to pay a minimal charge for a new driver's licence and you can ask your state to void your old licence number.
- If a credit card number has been stolen, you will only be liable for a minimum amount–as long as you report the crime in a timely fashion–and you should close the account immediately.
- If your financial information has been stolen, the amount you will be liable for will vary by the institution and the time you took to report the crime. You should close the account and consider opening an account with a different institution.

Plan ahead before you contact a credit company or financial institution regarding the theft of your identity. Make a list of the questions you want to ask. Do not assume the person you talk to will give you all the information you need. Stay on the phone until you are satisfied with the responses, and, if you are not satisfied, request to speak to a supervisor.

Do not dispose of your journal as soon as you believe your case has been settled. The results of identity theft can last for a long time, and you may be surprised when the theft causes you additional and unexpected problems at some point in the future.

How to Set-Up a System to Monitor Your Accounts and Finances

It is vital for you to monitor your finances whether you are a victim of financial theft or not. Sometimes you will not be able to discover illegal activity from simply reviewing a statement. You will need a system to keep track of what is going on with your accounts and what information the system you set-up can provide to you.

In addition to alerting you to fraud theft, setting-up a monitoring system can also help you keep track of the protective tools you use, such as the dates when fraud alerts expire or when anti-spyware software needs to be updated. The type of monitoring system that will work best for you will depend on what type of accounts you are dealing with and whether you prefer using a computer or printed documents. Either way, your monitoring system will be an essential part of your strategy to counteract identity theft.

Most of us believe we have no time to set-up a system of monitoring our finances, but this is not true. The time involved–after the initial set-up process–should not take more than an hour or two per month.

You can certainly set-up a system for monitoring your finances by using paper methods, such as notes, paper copies and ledger books. Many prefer to use computer programmes, which can be as simple as a spreadsheet or as sophisticated as a financial software management programme.

Managing your mail is an important part of setting-up a system of monitoring your accounts. Many people do not inspect their credit card accounts or financial statements until many days after they receive them. Many do not realise they are not receiving their bills, which could be an indication that their mail is being intercepted.

Part of monitoring your accounts involves chequeing your credit report on a regular schedule to discover signs of improper usage of your account. If you discover any unusual activity on your credit report, you can request a short-term fraud alert be placed on your account that will be in effect for 90 days. With proper proof from a police report, you can request a long-term fraud alert on your account that will last for up to 7 years. You can always remove

Learn Who to Contact if Something Goes Wrong

a fraud report from your credit report, if you believe there really has been no improper activity.

Properly monitoring your accounts is not just a fix-it measure for the effects of identity theft, it is also a preventive measure to allow you to know what is going on with your accounts for other purposes.

Part of monitoring your financial account is not simply looking over your information, but carefully tracking what information you can keep, what can be thrown away, and what is the best way to dispose of the information.

You do not have to wait for a paper copy of your credit card and financial statements to check and monitor your credit activity.

- Most financial institutions offer online banking services that will allow you to monitor your accounts whenever you go online. The activity you see will reflect activity up to the end of the last applicable business day. Some online services will allow you to see pending transactions and look at a copy of all cheques that have cleared.
- Almost all credit card companies will offer online services that allow you to view account activity, check your balance and even pay your bills online.
- If you are not that comfortable with computers, you can use your phone to check your current credit card or financial institution balances. However, usually you cannot access specific transactions via phone.

Some people may detect some unusual financial activity on their accounts–such as a series of small ATM withdrawals–that they will assume are simply small transactions they do not remember. Fraudsters will usually start by doing small, harder-to-detect thefts, and then later–if they believe they have not been detected–will increase the level of theft

Many financial institutions will offer a programme of action alerts if they detect what appears to be unusual activity on your account. Usually, these alerts will be part of your online banking services and sent to you via e-mail. This service may cost you an additional fee at your financial institution.

Placing a fraud alert on your accounts is not a guarantee that a thief may not open new credit or phone service under your name. Current law does not prohibit businesses opening new accounts just because a fraud alert has been placed on the credit report.

The Solutions

Being a victim of identity theft is a serious problem. But, if the remedy process helps you keep better track of your finances, you might at least feel as if something positive has happened from what is otherwise mostly a negative experience.

Learn Who to Contact if Something Goes Wrong 237

There are several important aspects of your finances that you should monitor on a regular basis and pay special attention to.

- Check to make sure your personal information is correct. This would include your name, address, marital status, National Insurance number and employment information. You may need to make a further follow-up if you see erroneous information suddenly appear on your financial reports.

- Make sure that every account you see listed on a credit report and the specific activities are correct. Examine the reports carefully.

- An important part of monitoring your credit report is to check for what inquiries were made to it. These may be the result of a fraudster using your information to open new accounts, new phone services or rent an apartment.

You can monitor your credit reports yourself, but you can also employ a commercial service. This may cost you some money but save you valuable time compared to doing the work yourself. A commercial service may be more diligent in checking your credit reports than you might be. Before you select a service, check them out with your local Better Business Bureau.

Go beyond just monitoring your accounts and do not hesitate to take action if you think something is wrong. It is better to be mistaken than to be further victimized.

Whether you do your own account monitoring by paper or by computer, there are certain activities that should be part of a clean credit checklist.

Weekly	Monthly	Annually
Go through all of your junk mail and shred all credit card applications.	Check your hard copy bank statement carefully. Shred all your ATM receipts. Store all canceled cheques in a safe place.	File the year's canceled cheques and bank statements in a safe place or shred them once you believe you no longer need them.
Go online and check your financial account activity.	Check your hard-copy credit card bill for any unusual activity. Check the statement against your receipts. Shred the receipts and save the statements in a safe place.	Shred all your credit card bills from the year, unless you believe they will be necessary for tax purposes or to combat a case of identity theft.

Weekly	Monthly	Annually
Make sure you received bills you would normally expect to receive during this period.	Review your cell phone and landline phone bills for suspicious usage involving calling cards.	Review all financial information you believe may be out of date and shred anything you do need.
	Update your virus protection software, anti-spyware software and firewalls.	Order your free credit report from one of the three major credit reporting bureaus and review it carefully for unauthorised activities.

Who Is Responsible for Losses When Theft Occurs?

While identity theft is, by itself, not a crime under UK law, misusing the identity information to fraudulently obtain goods or services is. Conservative estimates report that one in four individuals report that they have been a victim of identity theft in one form or another. Identity theft is growing at such an alarming rate that the Home Office passed new tough measures that could mean a fraudster could be arrested for merely possessing a false document. *The Identity Cards Act 2006* created offences relating to possession, control and intent to use false identity documents, including a genuine document that relates to someone else. These offences came into force on 7 June 2006 and apply to all identity documents, including identity cards to be issued under the National Identity Scheme. Other documents include UK passports, immigration documents and driving licences, as well as driving licences, passports and identity cards issued by other countries.

In addition, the Fraud Act 2006 came into force on 15 January 2007 and created a new offence of fraud that can be committed in three ways: by making a false representation (dishonestly, with intent to make a gain, cause loss or risk of loss to another), by failing to disclose information, and by abuse of position. Offences were also created of obtaining services dishonestly, possessing equipment to commit frauds, and making or supplying articles for use in frauds. This would mean that criminals who were caught with stolen documents–such as fake passports, or driving licences–could face up to

Learn Who to Contact if Something Goes Wrong

2 years in prison. The United States, which has also experienced a rapid rise in ID theft has already made it a crime under the *Identity Theft and Assumption Deterrence Act.*

The good news is that there are many types of theft that you will not be responsible for. But, unfortunately, there are some that you will find yourself carrying the burden for correcting. To help you combat an identity theft and spare you as much suffering as possible, you need to know what you have to do and what you can reasonably expect to get others to help you with.

Several aspects of combating identity theft are not strictly financial. For instance, the credit reporting bureaus can place fraud alerts on your credit reports, but they will not be able to reimburse you for any losses you may have incurred. Similarly, having your National Insurance number or driver's licence number stolen can result in a fraudster stealing your information to establish new identities and new accounts, but the theft of those numbers is not in and of itself a financial matter.

If your identity theft has gotten to the point where one of your credit accounts has been reported to a collection agency, that agency will not be responsible for any of your losses.

In most cases, credit card companies will limit

your liability to $50, but this varies by credit card company and how soon you report the suspected theft. The longer you wait, the less likely they will make up for the losses.

The responsibility for reimbursing you against losses from your financial protects you from improper transactions from your ATM or debit card. It also limits your liability. However, there are some requirements you must be aware of to give yourself some protection from identity theft to your financial accounts.

- You have 60 days from the date your bank account statement is sent to you–and you detect illegal activity–to report in writing any money you see has been withdrawn from your account without your knowledge or permission.
- If you report the loss within 2 business days of discovery, the losses are limited to $50.
- If you report the loss after 2 days but within 60 days after you receive the statement, your losses could cost you up to $500.
- If you wait more than 60 days after you receive the statement to report a loss, you could carry responsibility for the entire amount of the loss.

If someone who has stolen your identity has used it to declare bankruptcy under your name, you will be assuming the financial burden for correcting the problem.

Your misused identity may be used when the fraudster is involved in other criminal activity. This stolen information could result in you being charged fines that you have done nothing to incur, such as speeding tickets or other minor violations. You cannot be charged for a crime that you actually did not commit–but it may take some time to straighten matters out. Proof that your identity was stolen should be sufficient to be excused from minor legal matters.

A phone company should be able to remove any fraudulent charges on your bill once you have established that you are the victim of identity theft.

Fraudsters may open fraudulent student loans in your name and then default on those loans. You may be responsible for paying them, even if you did not take them out.

Some financial institutions may be willing to offer you a zero-liability guarantee that should protect you against most forms of financial fraud. You may have to pay a fee for this service, depending on the financial institution.

The Solutions

The key to limiting your financial liability following the theft of your identity is acting quickly when you suspect your identity has been misappropriated. The longer you wait, the more likely it is that you will pay more of the costs for the damage that has been done.

Know the rules before your report the crime. If you receive information that disputes what you have discovered by going online or reviewing your credit agreement, you need to communicate that.

Be aware of who you need to talk to when you report the identity theft. Get detailed information about what they can or cannot do to help you and what your expected losses can be. Refer to this when you continue the process of reporting the crime.

Follow up any communication in writing. Be sure to include the expected amount you will be liable for and why you believe this information is correct.

Escaping financial damages due to criminal activity can be a burden, but it has to be done.

If you receive tickets or notice of warrants of arrest, immediately contact the law enforcement agency that sent you the notice. Once you have shown the charges against you are due to identity theft, the law enforcement agency should recall any warrants or tickets and issue a clearance letter or certificate of release that should clear your record and free you from any fines from the criminal activity.

Learn Who to Contact if Something Goes Wrong 245

You may need to acquire a criminal lawyer to clear your name in any court records and freeing you from paying any fraudulently incurred fines or penalties.

You can stop a debt collector from trying to get money from you for debts you did not incur in two ways.

- Write a letter to the collection agency telling it to stop trying to collect the debt. The company cannot contact you again unless it tells you there will be no further action or it can tell you what specific action it will take against you.
- Send a letter within 30 days after you have received the notification telling the company you do not owe this money. Include all copies of any documentation that supports your case, including a police report. A debt collector can only resume collection activities if it sends you proof of the debt.

If a loss involves theft from a minor, you can contact the company involved and indicate the minor was not old enough to open a credit card account or legally incur the debt. This should limit any liability to your child or to you.

You have the right to all information regarding identity misuse. A company cannot refuse to give you this information if you ask for it in writing. However, in some cases a business may ask for proof of your identity and a police report or affidavit before releasing this information.

Expect that some of the losses you will incur from identity theft will not involve money out of your pocket. There will be time involved in resolving the problem, time that you might have to spend away from work. Part of the costs you will incur will be based on missed income and materials such as paper and postage.

Keep careful records of everything you are told about how much losses you will have to incur and how much the company will take care of. Take names. Record the dates and times of all conversations and be prepared to refer to them if needed.

Even if your financial loss is light, you will still likely suffer an emotional toll involved from this kind of theft. Unfortunately, this loss cannot be assumed by anybody but you, and you will find that it is important to deal with it–as well as the financial aspects–in order to consider the problem ultimately solved. Feeling an emotional hit is perfectly natural, and you cannot really put a price on it. By taking action and following through with all of your points of contact, you can reduce both types of loss.

Identity Theft Affidavit

Consumers victimized by identity theft used to have to fill out a variety of forms, each one in a different format and requesting different information. If you are a victim of identity theft, you need to know what an Identity Theft Affidavit can do to help you and how to accurately fill one out.

The Identity Theft Affidavit was developed to streamline the process by which victims report an identity theft to credit card companies and financial institutions. The Identity Theft Affidavit allows those victims to fill out one, standardized form rather than many different forms, each one created by and for only one specific company. Once you begin to think about the number of credit card companies and financial institutions you conduct business with, you will realise how much paperwork the affidavit could save you.

However, the Identity Theft Affidavit is not a perfect solution-merely a help-because it is not mandatory that companies use it. Many do, but you may also encounter companies that still opt to use their own forms for the reporting of identity theft.

An Identity Theft Affidavit is not the same as a police report. However, completing an Identity

Theft Affidavit may help you in filling out a police report.

Also, do not use the Identity Theft Affidavit to file a report with other government agencies. These agencies have their own specific requirements based on how they will use the information, and the Identity Theft Affidavit was not designed to meet those needs.

In the first part of an Identity Theft Affidavit, you provide general information about yourself and the theft.

- Your legal name
- Birthday
- National Insurance number
- Driver's licence or state ID number
- Current address and how long you have lived there
- Your address, if different, when the theft took place and how long you lived at that location
- Daytime and evening telephone numbers
- A checklist on how you believe the fraud occurred
- Whether you have reported the crime to police or are willing to prosecute the crime
- Supporting documentation including a copy of your driver's licence or NI card and a copy of a proof of residence, such as a lease, utility bill or insurance bill

Learn Who to Contact if Something Goes Wrong 249

The second part of the Identity Theft Affidavit is called a fraudulent account statement and is the section in which you will detail the identity theft-related information pertaining to each individual company. In this section, you describe the specific fraudulent accounts opened in your name.

- Creditor name and address
- Credit or financial account number
- Type of unauthorised–if you know–credit, goods or services provided by the creditor
- Date account issued
- The amount of the unauthorised usage of the account
- Your billing name and address

If a business opts to have you use its own forms rather than the Identity Theft Affidavit, the report will usually include two parts:(1) a copy of a police report filed by you and (2) information that is specifically required by the company you are reporting the theft to. Depending on the company, the information required could be extensive.

A business that requires its own reporting forms be used rather than an Identity Theft Affidavit must inform you of this within 15 days of when you make the initial contact to report the suspected fraud. The consumer reporting agency or company then has 15 more days to work with your regarding properly reporting the theft. They can take 5 days to review any of the information you have sent them.

If you notice unauthorised activities on existing accounts, contact that company's fraud or security department and ask if they will accept the Identity Theft Affidavit. However, assume that you will need to file an Identity Theft Affidavit with any companies that have opened new credit as a result of the fraudulent use of our identification. The information will be used to help these companies investigate new accounts and validate your claim.

The Solutions

Do not assume that all companies affected by your identity theft will accept the Identity Theft Affidavit. You must determine this by contacting the company through its fraud and security office. If the company will not accept the Identity Theft Affidavit, it will need to provide you with its own reporting forms either by mail, fax or through a secure online form.

Even if the individual company will not take the Identity Theft Affidavit, by filling out the form before you start reporting the fraudulent activity, you may be able to better ogranise your information and as a result find it easier to fill out any other individual reports.

Learn Who to Contact if Something Goes Wrong

In addition to filling out an Identity Theft Affidavit, you still need to follow other avenues of reporting identity theft.

- You should report the suspected theft to any of the three credit reporting agencies. If you report the crime to one, the other two will also be alerted to the crime. The agency may accept an Identity Theft Affidavit or require you to fill out a separate form.

- You may choose to close compromised accounts and open new accounts with different passwords and PINs.

- You should file a complaint with your local law enforcement agencies.

Before you submit an Identity Theft Affidavit, review the disputed accounts with a trusted family member or friend, especially one who has information about or access to them. You may discover you have left out important information that will help resolve your problem.

Never send originals as attachments to the Identity Theft Affidavit. If you are required to send a police report or personal identification, always send copies of these.

Keep all copies of your Identity Theft Affidavits in your identity theft file and attach notes to them indicating when you sent them and what follow-up action was taken by the companies you sent them to.

If you suspect identity theft has compromised your accounts, complete the Identity Theft Affidavit as soon as possible. Many credit companies and financial institutions will require you to send this within 2 weeks of your initial contact with them. If you delay filling out the application, it can significantly slow down the process of investigating your claims.

The Identity Theft Affidavit has a space on each page for your name and phone number. Make sure you fill this information out on every page in case the pages of the document become separated.

Only attach the fraudulent account statement to the Identity Theft Affidavit for the specific company you are sending it to. You do not need to send copies of the fraudulent account statements you put together for all the companies but rather only the one that pertains to that company.

Send the Identity Theft Affidavit and any supporting documents to the specific company by certified mail with a return receipt required or by a commercial shipping company that will provide a tracking number. Later you may need to verify or document that the package was received, by whom and when.

Completing an Identity Theft Affidavit is no guarantee that the fraudster will be caught and arrested. It is simply a means to alert companies that you believe there is fraudulent activity on your accounts.

In most cases, the information you provide on an Identity Theft Affidavit will only be seen and used by the specific company you send it to for investigating the suspected fraud. However, if a lawsuit results from your case, the company may have to provide the information to the other party in the suit.

In the case of a minor or someone who is unable to complete the Identity Theft Affidavit, a legal guardian or someone with power of attorney can complete it and submit it to the company.

Remedying Identity Theft Problems

Much of the effort you put into correcting the effects of identity theft will involve writing letters and filling out forms. In this chapter you will find some of the most commonly forms and letters used to help combat identity theft. Remember, make sure all of your letters look original, not written by a third party such as a lawyer or credit counseling service. Change the language as much as possible to customize it to your situation.

Keep copies of all your letters and forms in files set-up by logical categories so you can always easily reference them, especially during a phone call.

When you send letters and forms, do so by certified mail so that you will receive proof of receipt.

Also included here are charts and checklists to determine how vulnerable you may be to identity theft and what actions you need to take once you realise your identity has been compromised.

Statement	Score	Points Scored
I limit the number of cards with identifying information.	5 points if you have less than five cards. 0 points if you have more than 10 cards.	
I do not carry my Social Security Card in my wallet or billfold.	5 points if you do not. 0 points if you do.	

Statement	Score	Points Scored
I carry my National Insurance card only when I need it.	5 points if you do only carry your NI card if you need it. 2 points if you carry your NI Card. 20 points if your insurance company has issued you a card without your National Insurance number on it.	
I have checked my driver's licence and it does not show my National Insurance number.	5 points if your licence does not show your National Insurance number. 10 points if your have a new licence with a substitute number.	
My National Insurance number does not appear on my bank cheques.	5 points if your National Insurance number does not appear.	

256 How to Protect Yourself from Identity Theft

Score: Above 20 means you are reducing your risk of identity theft and guarding your National Insurance number.

Below 20 means you need to work on guarding your identity.

Clean Credit Checklist

Weekly	Monthly	Annually
Go through *junk mail* and shred all credit card applications.		
	Check bank statements. Destroy all ATM receipts. Save canceled cheques in a safe place.	File canceled cheques and bank statements in a safe place.
	Check credit card bills against receipts. Shred receipts and save statements in safe place.	Shred credit card bills unless you need them for tax purposes.

Weekly	Monthly	Annually
	Check cell phone and calling card bills for evidence of suspicious use.	Shred any out-of-date financial information.
	Download latest virus protection software.	Order credit reports from any of the three national credit reporting bureaus.

Protect Your Physical Space

All outside doors	Use metal or solid wood with a single- or double-cylinder deadbolt lock.
Front doors	Make sure glass panels, mail slots and pet doors are at least 36 inches from doorknob.
Sliding glass doors	Install screws in the track above the sliding part. Install a *Charley Bar*, a solid bar that secures in place between the sliding door and frame. (Or, you can use a piece of wood in the inside track so the door will not open.)

French doors	Install heavy-duty vertical bolts to secure the doors at top and bottom along with a deadbolt to latch the doors together.
Windows	Install secure locks and window stops on all windows accessible from the ground, trees, ledges, balconies and rooftops.
Garage doors	These are usually the weakest point in home security, especially those with electronic garage door openers. Install a solid, windowless outside entry door to the garage in a location where it cannot be easily seen. Install a solid entry door from your garage to your home, and always lock your car.
Entry to attic or crawl space	Use sturdy padlocks or consider having openings professionally sealed.

Checklist for Identity Theft Case Log

Case Log	Keep a *dated* log on your computer or on a ledger.

Journaling	Keep track of each person you speak with including their title, employee phone number, phone and fax numbers, e-mail addresses and how you can reach them. Make notes on what is said, and what you need to do for any follow-up.
Confirm agreements and discussions	When possible, ask for a written confirmation of your discussion. If that is refused, send your own *Confirmation of Discussion* by certified mail and ask for it to be signed off on.
Log items	Keep track of what you have sent, who you sent it to and when it was received.
Telephone records	Create a separate address and telephone book, separate from the case log to help you reach anyone you have dealt with.
Costs	Keep a log of every amount of money you have spent–including phone calls, postage, mileage, professional assistance and time spent away from work–and save this for future court actions regarding liability for a company which has allowed your identity to be stolen.

Letter of Victim Summary or Narrative

Name:

Date of Birth:

Driver's Licence Number:

National Insurance number:

Home Address:

Home Phone Number:

E-mail address:

Best time to reach you:

Discovery of Fraud

On date I received a call from company and representative name that I owe amount of money and the account has been sold to his or her collection agency. I told him or her of why I do not know about this debt. I was told I would receive a letter in the mail.

Activity to Date in Chronological Order

On date I did this and was told of this response.

Repeat as needed.

Affected Accounts

List separately each account name and number and the amount owed to date.

Facts About the Imposter

List why you believe your information was stolen; or describe why you do not know how information was stolen but list all the latest applications for credit or an apartment you have done in the last three months.

Quote a representative from a financial institution officer detailing how the theft might have occurred.

Model Letter to Place Fraud Alert on Credit Reports for Compromised National Insurance number

Date:

Dear:

I am contacting you about a potential problem involving identity theft. Describe the information compromised and what you are doing to respond to it.

Please place a fraud alert on your credit file. This fraud alert tells creditors to contact you before they open any new accounts or change existing accounts. As soon as one credit bureau confirms the fraud alert, the others should be notified and I should be sent credit reports to me free of charge.

If you find suspicious activity on your credit reports or have reason to believe my information is being misused, please contact appropriate law enforcement agency.

Sign with your name.

The Good and Bad of Changing Your National Insurance Number

One of the most important parts of your identity is your National Insurance number. Often you will be asked for this number to establish credit, rent an apartment or establish phone service. There are also occasions when you should not give out your National Insurance number, such as at a doctor or dentist's office.

But, if your National Insurance number has been stolen what should you do? You can get a new National Insurance number, but there can be serious repercussions if you do. You need to know what affect it will have if you change your National Insurance number and, also, what you will need to do to establish a new National Insurance number.

A new National Insurance number will not put an end to a poor credit record. Your credit information is tied to your name (and/or your spouse's name), not just to your National Insurance number. The credit bureaus will likely match your name and your spouse's name attached to your new National Insurance number and combine it with the information connected to your old number.

A National Insurance number is a major entry point to your identity. Therefore, the Department for Work and Pensions (DWP) needs to know when your National Insurance number has been stolen, even if you do not want to acquire a new NI number.

Your stolen number could be used by illegal immigrants or terrorists to represent falsely themselves as legal residents of the United Kingdom. A stolen National Insurance number can also be useful to thieves who are trying to avoid paying income taxes.

There are several examples of common misuse of National Insurance numbers by criminals:

- Applying for credit using your National Insurance number.
- Applying for an apartment or a job using your National Insurance number.
- Giving out your National Insurance number to a law enforcement official.
- Using your National Insurance number to discover your location for the purposes of harassment or abuse.

There are several examples of what might appear to be National Insurance number abuse but are not.

- A landlord using your National Insurance number to check your credit history or check to see if you have a criminal record.

Learn Who to Contact if Something Goes Wrong 265

- Applying for credit using your name but not your National Insurance number.
- Furnishing your name, but not your National Insurance number, to a law enforcement official.
- A credit reporting bureau using your National Insurance number as an identifier.

National Insurance numbers are a matter of public record, especially in the cases of property transactions. This number can be acquired through legal measures and still be misappropriated.

You will have to follow strict DWP guidelines if you decide to change your National Insurance number. In general, experts recommend against changing your National Insurance number, mainly because a changed number will separate you from scholastic and financial records that were established under your original number.

Changing your National Insurance number is no guarantee that it will be invulnerable. You will need to take the same, basic steps to protect your new National Insurance number that you would have taken to continue to protect the old one.

Getting a new National Insurance number will not speed along the process of repairing the effects of your identity theft. In many cases, it may not have any effect at all on the process.

You must not rush to get a new National Insurance number if you think improper activity has appeared on your credit report. Almost one-third of all credit reports contain misinformation that has nothing to do with identity theft and does not involve a stolen National Insurance number. This misinformation is usually due to human error in entering numbers or other data.

Having a new National Insurance number may cause you problems because it may appear that you have no credit history. This lack of credit history could limit your ability to be granted new credit or a loan.

However, there are some exceptions to the recommendations not to change your National Insurance number.

- If you are just starting out in life and have not established a credit history. This is especially true when a minor is the victim of identity theft.
- If the theft of your National Insurance number could have life-threatening implications and has been strongly suggested by government or local law enforcement agencies.
- Your identity theft case is so extreme that a lawyer with proven experience in identity theft cases recommends you take this action.

If you do change your National Insurance number, the DWP will not destroy or reassign your old

National Insurance number. This information will be used to cross-reference your new number.

The Solutions

A request to change your National Insurance number must be approved by your central DWP office. You cannot change your National Insurance number without this approval. To get this approval, you must provide proof that your stolen National Insurance number will cause damage in your personal life or your financial life.

You must apply in person for a new National Insurance number at your local DWP office. You cannot do this by mail, over the phone or online. The DWP officials at the office will help you complete an application and a statement explaining why you need a new National Insurance number.

You should request that the DWP send you a letter indicating that your National Insurance number was changed due to your belief that your original number was misused. This letter can later be used to help you apply for new credit.

Once you are assigned a new National Insurance number, you should not use your old National Insurance number under any circumstances. Use of the old number could be an indicator of fraudulent activity on your financial accounts–unless you muddy the waters by using it, too.

You need to alert anyone who is legally using your original National Insurance number that you have a new National Insurance number. This could include your financial institutions, your landlord, your employer and the IRS.

Hiring a Lawyer

Although much of the work that needs to be done to remedy the effects of identity theft will have to be done by you alone, you can also seek professional advice while working through the sometimes-lengthy process. For instance, the advice of local law enforcement and other government officials can be helpful and will likely not cost you anything other than the time you spend talking with them.

However, in some cases, you may wish to hire a lawyer with a background in identity theft cases to work with you. As with securing the services of any professional, you will want to make sure you have selected a person with the right credentials and are getting the best return on your investment. It is important that you know what a lawyer can do to help you in the event of identity theft and how to choose the right person to work with.

Most of the problems associated with identity theft will involve your having to contact credit

Learn Who to Contact if Something Goes Wrong 269

bureaus, and the credit and financial institutions, telephone companies and other companies that are the common targets of fraudsters. However, should certain types of issues rise, it might be best to secure the services of a lawyer. Examples of issues that indicate the need for a lawyer include:

- The existence of criminal actions against you as a result of misappropriation of your identity;
- a desire to file lawsuits against your employer or a company you believe was negligent in guarding your identity;
- the need for help preparing information for police reports;
- your need for representation in cases of a false bankruptcy filed under your name; and
- your need for someone to work with on legal matters resulting from mortgage theft.

Although a lawyer can be of help with many aspects of an identity theft case, one of the most important may be to represent you in court regarding legal action taken mistakenly against you. You could become involved in a wrongful criminal case as a result of identity theft in one of two ways:

- The fraudster is cited for a traffic or misdemeanor violation, provides your identity to the officer and is released and ordered to appear in court. The fraudster does not make that court appearance, and so an arrest warrant is issued against you.

- If the fraudster does appear in court and is convicted using your name, this information may be filed in county, state or federal databases. The fraudster is eventually released with no criminal record, while you are now listed as a convicted criminal.

You may have already used the services of a lawyer for such matters as estate planning, purchasing real estate or filing lawsuits. While it may be tempting to work with a lawyer you already know, it is quite possible that he or she does not have the background necessary to best represent you when it comes to a case of identity theft issues. Do not hesitate to ask your lawyer about this, and, if you are not satisfied by the answers he or she provides, ask for a referral. Sometimes the referral may be to a lawyer in the same firm.

You probably will not be able to sue any institution or company for liability and losses due to the theft of your identity if you yourself were negligent in maintaining security. This would include responding to scam e-mails or phone calls, having your property stolen, getting your mail intercepted or not properly shredding sensitive documents before putting them in the trash.

While a lawyer can help you with liability lawsuits or by defending you in court in any illegal actions of a fraudster using your name, a private attorney cannot bring criminal actions against any identity theft perpetrators. Criminal actions can only be brought by the appropriate law enforcement agencies and your district attorney's office.

In the case of criminal action against you based on misappropriation of your identity, you should work with your lawyer to establish aggressively your innocence. Establish an alibi by providing your date book, employment records or receipts indicating where you actually were when the crime was committed. Request that the physical description of the perpetrator be compared to your physical description. In the case of a misdemeanor that may not involve a detailed description or fingerprints, ask the police to compare your signature with that of the perpetrator's on the violation ticket.

The Solutions

There are several ways to find a lawyer who may be able to help you with identity theft cases.

- Ask for referrals from local law enforcement officials.
- See if any of your friends or family can refer you to a qualified attorney.

Before you retain a lawyer in this situation, you need to be thorough in checking out his or her background and experience in handling the type of case you have. There are certain questions you need to ask.

- What professional experience do you have dealing with identity theft issues?
- How many identity theft cases have you successfully worked on?
- Are you certified by any professional organisations for these types of cases?
- What are your fees, whether a flat fee or an hourly rate?
- What can I reasonably expect to pay in total for my case?
- How fast do you return phone calls?
- Will you be working on my case or will the work actually be done by someone else in your firm?
- Can you provide references related to the work you have done on identity theft related cases?

In most circumstances, it will cost you some money to hire a lawyer. Fees will vary depending on the attorney and what he or she perceives as the scope of the work. If you purchase identity theft insurance, this insurance may reimburse you for the legal fees incurred. You also may be able to find a lawyer willing to handle your case for no fee, or pro bono. Also, some communities have legal clinics that will provide services for free or for a nominal fee.

You may be tempted to ask a lawyer to prepare letters and fraud alerts to be sent out regarding your suspicion of identity theft. However, in most cases, you should prepare these documents yourself and avoid having a second party sign these letters. Credit bureaus and financial institutions and credit card companies might ignore any letter they perceive as being a form letter, or they may even refer the report to their security department.

Cleaning Up Your Credit Report

The long-term effects of identity theft could involve major damage to your credit reports. Fraudsters can open new accounts in your name and not make payments on them–including car loans and credit cards–and the information about these illegal activities will find its way into your credit report and can have a negative affect on your credit history.

After you have discovered the identity theft, you can take action to clean up your credit report, but you must expect this to take some time, work and, in many cases, repeated efforts, to clear your credit. You need to know how you can dispute inaccurate or fraudulent activities on your report as well as have reasonable expectations as to what your actions can accomplish. You will discover that cleaning up your credit report can be a complicated and frustrating process, but with the right information and a determined attitude, you can be successful.

Credit reporting bureaus are required to respond to your requests to change information on the report based on your belief your identity has been stolen.

One aspect of cleaning up your credit report is disputing any requests for credit information appearing on your credit report that you did not initiate. There are two ways to dispute false information in your credit report. These are:

- Writing a letter of dispute with any supporting documents.
- Filling out the Consumer Statement in your credit report and returning it to the credit reporting bureau.

If a credit reporting bureau decides that the point you make in your dispute is correct, the bureau must delete the information from your files in a timely manner. If the agency cannot decide if your dispute is correct within a reasonable time, it will still have to delete the information from the files.

If you do challenge an item on your credit report, the credit reporting agency must confirm the disputed information within 30 days of receiving notice of the dispute from you. Be prepared to send them a reminder letter if you do not receive a response within that time period.

Fixing your credit report will filter down to the people who have made recent inquiries on your

Learn Who to Contact if Something Goes Wrong 275

credit when you have successfully disputed any erroneous information on your credit report caused by identity theft. Under federal law, a credit agency must send a free notification of any corrections to any company or individual who has received a copy of the erroneous report within 6 months previous to any corrections made to the report. Sometimes credit reporting bureaus will simply send out revised credit reports to all companies or individuals who have made recent inquiries.

Sometimes an incorrect item on your credit report will be removed without you having to prove it is incorrect. If you challenge an individual item and the company involved does not follow up on the challenge, the item should be removed from your credit report. Often smaller companies will not bother to respond to challenges, and so the incorrect information will typically be removed from your report due to this lack of response.

Correcting erroneous information on your credit report that resulted from identity theft will not remedy damage done to individual accounts or problems resulting from any false identities set-up in your name for illegal purposes. Also, if you first became aware of the identity theft as a result of being contacted by a debt collection agency, you will still need to deal with that agency as well as the company that hired them. You will still have to work with the proper governmental agencies and your individual financial institutions to remedy these problems.

The Solutions

You can challenge any incorrect information on your credit report. Just because it appears on your report does not mean it is accurate. Usually you will have to report an error in writing rather than by phone, fax or e-mail. You can send the credit bureau a letter or you can use the consumer statement section of the report to challenge any information in your credit report. If you use the Consumer Statement section, your challenge is limited to 100 words or fewer.

Credit repair services offer form letters for correcting incorrect information on your credit report. However, credit reporting bureaus will often not respond to requests that look like they were generated by a credit counseling agency. Sometimes, they will even forward these letters to their security departments. Either way, you will likely be more successful in challenging incorrect information on your credit report if you send a hand-written letter or, at least, one that is clearly an original letter written by you.

When you write your letter of dispute, use firm but polite language when you list what items need to be changed and why you believe they should be changed. You may have to provide backup documentation to have items changed, including an Identity Theft Affidavit or police report. You do not have to go into extensive detail about why the item is incorrect. It is the responsibility of the company listing the item to verify that the information is correct.

If you are self-employed and your employment history is included on your credit report, the report may list you as unemployed. You must challenge this information in the same way you would challenge any other inaccurate information on your credit report.

Sometimes it is possible to eliminate inaccuracies in your credit report simply by making the effort to dispute them. The major credit reporting bureaus are required to investigate your claims of fraudulent or disputed activity on your credit report, but sometimes the company in question fails to respond to the credit bureau's enquiry. In these cases, the credit bureau will usually update your credit report so that it is consistent with the statement it received from you.

If you challenge any aspect of your credit report, request a new copy of the credit report 30 to 45 days after making your challenge, and check the report thoroughly. Although you are likely to be charged a small fee for this second copy of the report, it is important that you confirm that the corrections you requested have actually been made.

Be prepared to be persistent in correcting your credit information. It is not uncommon for credit reporting bureaus to delay or automatically deny a dispute. If you hear nothing from them, send follow-up letters or make follow-up phone calls.

You can do more than just dispute an item on your credit report. Credit bureaus must send notices of any corrections to anyone who received your report in the past 6 months. In addition, if your credit report had been supplied to prospective employers in the past 2 years, you can have corrected copies of your report sent to those companies as well.

Follow the other guidelines in remedying identity theft when you are cleaning up your credit report. Keep a file of all your correspondence, and send any letters as certified mail with a return receipt.

Do not be tempted to clean up your credit by destroying all your credit cards and not applying for future credit or loans. If you have no current credit history, this can affect your getting a necessary loan or even leasing an apartment. New lenders or landlords may consider a lack of credit history to be just as risky as a bad credit history.

Even though, with knowledge of your legal rights and some hard work, you can do a lot to repair your credit yourself, some consumers who have encountered credit problems as a result of identity theft are turning to professional counsellors. After reviewing your individual circumstances, a credit counseling agency may suggest you enroll in a debt management plan (DMP). Under a DMP, you deposit money each month with the credit counseling company. The organisation then uses your money to pay your unsecured debts. However, these plans are not for everyone.

If you decide to use a credit counseling agency, try to find one that offers in-person counseling. Your bank or local consumer protection agency may offer referrals to reputable agencies. You can also find non-profit credit counseling agencies through universities, state cooperative extension offices, military bases, and credit unions and housing authorities.

A credit counseling agency must know the details of your particular case of identity theft. Your having been a victim of identity theft will affect how they help you deal with your problem. You must be prepared to provide back-up information such as identity theft affidavits or police reports to prove the credit problems are due to identity theft.

A Final Word

There are a number of useful and hopefully helpful suggestions about how you can prevent identity theft from happening to you or, at the very least, help you repair damage that may be caused by identity thieves. As identity theft becomes more prevalent, you can take solace in the fact that it is an indiscriminate crime. If you do find your identity has been stolen by a fraudster, do not be discouraged, here in this book you have the tools to tackle this problem head-on.

Some of the information presented in this book is just basic common sense, while other information is...eye-opening. But there is one thing for sure, if you follow the sound advice presented in this book, you will increase your chances of keeping your personal information safe and secure! So go about shopping, traveling and paying your bills online with confidence and know you are taking every protective measure to keep your information safe.

INDEX

911
  emergency services 52

account
  checking 6, 61, 175
  compromised 222
  credit card 28, 30, 32, 94, 245
  financial 99, 102, 110, 117, 179, 219, 224, 235, 238, 249
  ISP 218
  savings 117, 153

adware 46, 47, 49, 50, 64, 73, 76, 77, 78, 79, 80, 81, 82

Apple iTunes 48

application backdoors 171

auction 59, 84, 209

automatice teller machine (ATM) 10, 13, 41, 43, 92, 97, 98, 102, 147, 149, 150, 176, 177, 179, 236, 238, 242, 256

bank 1, 2, 7, 8, 11, 15, 16, 18, 24, 30, 40, 44, 65, 71, 72, 76, 92, 104, 109, 113, 118, 147, 148, 150, 178, 238, 242, 255, 256, 279

bankruptcy
  fraud 129, 130, 132

Better Business Bureau 95, 202, 237

botnets 73, 83, 87

brokerage 17

cell phone 86, 88, 92, 115, 168, 239, 257

Chex Systems, Inc 102

clean credit checklist 238

clearance letter 244

collection letter 23, 225

credit
  bureau 23, 120, 152, 156, 159, 163, 164, 165, 192, 193, 196, 198, 209, 210, 263, 268
  cards 6, 7, 8, 11, 13, 14, 15, 17, 24, 28, 30, 31, 33, 40, 71, 92, 97, 103, 116, 131, 136, 139, 141, 143, 146, 148, 149, 153, 166, 218, 273, 278
  cleaning up 119, 273, 276, 278
  history 30, 37, 125, 156, 264, 268, 273, 278

management services 197
monitoring services 194, 196
pre-approved 30, 66, 117, 118
report 13, 21, 29, 33, 38, 74, 100, 108, 117, 120, 152, 153, 154, 155, 156, 157, 162, 165, 166, 178, 190, 193, 196, 197, 198, 199, 210, 213, 220, 236, 235, 236, 237, 239, 266, 273, 274, 275, 276, 277, 278
reporting bureaus 37, 117, 131, 133, 157, 164, 167, 168, 190, 193, 196, 197, 199, 206, 207, 208, 212, 213, 217, 220, 226, 239, 241, 257, 275, 276, 277, 278
report requests 153
reviewing 176
score 6, 152, 154, 197
unauthorized 6, 15, 17, 31, 33, 35, 41, 44, 66, 114, 115, 130, 144, 146, 147, 150, 151, 160, 170, 171, 206, 219, 220, 222, 223, 239, 249, 250

debit card 102, 146, 177

debt management plan (DMP) 279

denial of service 172

domain name server 88

dumpster diving 7

e-mail bombs 172

eBay 59, 84

electronic check conversion 149

employment 38, 106, 152, 237, 271, 277

encryption 39, 41, 42, 43, 60, 101, 150, 180

End User License Agreement (EULA) 34, 43, 47, 78, 80, 81

Equifax 196

Federal Trade Commission (FTC) 203, 215, 247, 249, 250

file sharing 45, 46, 48, 49, 82

file transfer protocol (FTP) 84, 87, 88

financial software management program 234

firewall 13, 44, 46, 74, 80, 82, 87, 170, 173, 239

fraud
alert 164, 165, 166, 167, 168, 169, 193, 206, 213, 226, 234, 236, 262
financial 100, 243
Internet 10
mortgage 123, 124, 125, 126
telephone 8

fraudulent account statement 249, 252

freeware 77, 78, 81

hyperlink 80

identity theft
affidavit 212, 214, 216, 247, 248, 249, 250, 251, 252, 253, 277
business 111
insurance 158, 159, 160, 161, 162, 163, 164, 195, 198, 272

journal 2225
of children 117

international driver's license 142, 144

Internet Service Provider (ISP) 41, 79, 88, 92, 93, 94, 180, 218

Kazaa P2P 49

lawsuit 253, 269, 270

local area network (LAN) 45, 114, 172

macros 171

magnetic information character recognition code (MICR) 101

malware 85, 87

monitoring system 233

MyDoom virus 49

Napster 48

notary 231

online banking 17, 35, 39, 40, 41, 42, 43, 101, 148, 235, 236

opt-out 38

passport 110, 134, 135, 136, 137, 138, 139, 140, 141, 142, 143, 146, 205, 214

password 10, 12, 14, 40, 44, 59, 62, 74, 77, 78, 99, 101, 107, 113, 114, 150, 159, 175, 176, 177, 178, 179, 180, 181, 251

Peer-to-Peer (P2P) 45, 46, 47, 48, 49, 50, 51, 78, 81

personal identification number (PIN) 102, 147, 149, 178, 179

phishing
e-mail 56
spear 71

phone tree 29, 55, 100, 207, 209

police report 135, 139, 159, 205, 214, 216, 217, 220, 222, 224, 226, 227, 234, 245, 247, 248, 249, 25`, 277

post office 11, 18, 19, 137

pre-texting 9, 73, 95, 100, 108, 115

privacy
policy 34, 35, 36, 37, 38, 59
protection 196

remote login 171

rootkits 85

scams
check overpayment 66
debt relief 67
e-mail 63, 64, 67, 74
fake survey 64
foreign lottery 65
Nigerian 64
pay-in-advance credit offer 66
scholarship 67, 118
weight loss 65
work-at-home 65

secure socket layer 42

shoulder surfing 179

skimming 125

SMTP session hijacking 171

snoopware 77

social security
  administration 106, 108, 204, 264, 265, 266, 267
  card 254
  children's 103
  new 111, 159, 232, 263, 264, 265, 266, 267, 268
  number 7, 8, 11, 12, 13, 14, 37, 61, 63, 64, 70, 71, 92, 93, 94, 96, 102, 103, 104, 105, 106, 107, 108, 109, 110, 114, 117, 119, 120, 122, 130, 133, 146, 152, 156, 159, 160, 165, 177, 179, 192, 213, 226, 232, 237, 241, 249, 263, 264, 265, 266, 267, 268

software
  anti-virus 74, 85, 172
  malicious 71, 85, 87
  unwanted 76, 78, 82, 81

spam filter 68

Spam Over Internet Telephony (SPIT) 53, 54

spyware 10, 36, 41, 44, 46, 47, 49, 50, 53, 64, 68, 73, 76, 77, 78, 79, 80, 81, 82, 83, 85, 86, 94, 99, 114, 170, 182, 183, 236, 239

Taxpayer Identification Number (TIN) 109, 110, 112, 113

theft
  mortgage 123, 124, 269

toner phoners 110

TransUnion 196

Trojan horse 77, 85

TRUSTe 61

U.S. Trustee Field office 133

Voice over Internet Protocol (VoIP) 51, 52, 53, 54, 55, 56, 57

warrant 244, 269

warrants 269